All rights reserved. No part of this book may be reproduced or used in any manner without the prior written permission of the copyright owner, except for the use of brief quotations in a book review. Copyright © 2022 Neti Neti Inc. No portion of this book may be reproduced in any form without permission from the publisher, except as permitted by U.S. copyright law.

For permissions
contact: info@ netinetiinc.com
or visit: www.netinetipublishing.com

Thank you for buying one of our products. Please visit our website for information on all our other products

www.netinetipublishing.com

This Journal Belongs to

Name ....

Gifted by ....

Date ....

Sentiments ....

....

....

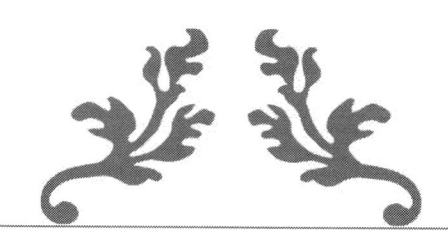

SURVIVING THE BREAKUP AND PREVENTING OTHERS

DENISE DIXON

Copyright © 2022 Denise Dixon

All rights reserved. No part of this book may be reproduced or used in any manner without the prior written permission of the copyright owner, except for the use of brief quotations in a book review.

Copyright © 2022 Neti Neti Inc and Denise Dixon.

No portion of this book may be reproduced in any form without permission from the publisher, except as permitted by U.S. copyright law.

For permissions contact:
https://www.netinetipublishing.com

Dedication

This book is dedicated to you, the reader. I dedicate this book to you because of your courage to go boldly where you could have avoided: within. The same actions over and over again are likely not going to yield a different outcome. Change is the only way to change. Your purchase of this workbook is already a step in a new direction.

Relationships can be challenging, but self-awareness is a helpful tool to navigate these obstacles. This book will challenge you, push you to examine yourself, reflect on your choices in partners, identify your blind spots and reconcile your vision for the relationship you want, need and deserve.

It is easy to want the best, but always remember that which you want, you must be willing to give and be as well. This book was written to help you take a closer look at your wants, needs and desires from a partner. It was also written with the intention of challenging you to look at who you bring to your relationships, what parts of you are seen and unseen and compromises you may or may not make.

When you ask yourself some of the questions in this workbook and consider some of the answers, you will become more aware, make better choices and most importantly, identify and recognize aspects of yourself that may need to be accepted, rejected, adjusted, cemented and/or explored.

That which you seek is also seeking you, but you must be the person that is deserving of that, willing to reciprocate, willing to go beyond your emotional comfort into emotional healing so you can first be that which you want someone to be for you.

I am honored to take this journey with you. In the words of Aristotle "Knowing yourself is the beginning of all wisdom." As we explore the terrains of your relationship landscapes, let us dive deep into that which is our birthright: to be happy, fulfill and congruent.

Acknowledgments

I am so grateful to have people in my life who always encourage me to follow my dreams, no matter how big or small. As I embark on this next chapter of my life, know that I take you all with me in my heart and with my dreams. I could not have been so brave to pursue this dream had it not been for the following:

꙳ MOM ꙳

You are the definition of survival, strength, joy, and support.

You never had all you needed, but you did the best with what you had. You live your life, enjoying the big and small moments. The way you live is an example that reminds me to smell the roses. I love you.

꙳ WENDY ꙳

I would not be the woman I am today without you.

You are such an incredible sister, and a better friend, I could never ask for.

"Com yah mi sista"

You are brave, strong, incredible and a force to be reckoned with. You make every day a little easier to navigate, enjoy and laugh at. I love you.

꙳ NIKKI ꙳

You are one of the funniest people I know

you always help me find a way to laugh at myself. You are just as resourceful as you say I am, so never forget that.

Thanks for being a cheerleader. I love you.

ᘍ MARVIN, OLISHA AND OLIVER ᘌ

My big brothers and my little sister

I appreciate you and all the steps you take in your daily lives, eating your elephants one bite at a time while being incredible siblings and human beings.

I love you.

ᘍ NAHOMIE ᘌ

You have been a pillar of support that words could never express enough gratitude for, but thank you for all you do, and who you are.

I love you.

ᘍ AUNTY PAM ᘌ

You are the closest person I know to a Saint. Your unconditional love and support for me and our entire family will never be forgotten. I love you.

ᘍ MAURICE ᘌ

Maurice thank you for being such an incredible part of our lives these last few years. You are an incredible person, and we appreciate you immensely.

⊱ ALL OTHER FAMILY MEMBERS ⊰

May we continue to break cycles and generational curses, move the needle leaps and bounds, while propelling the next generation beyond our wildest dreams.

I am so proud of the progress we've made. Those who we have loved and lost, are still with us. We carry some of their hopes and dreams across the finish line. I thank you for your love and support and I don't take for granted, the shoulders I stand on or the ones that pushed me to the ground.

⊱ DENNIS AND HARI ⊰

you restored my faith in the existence of unconditional love You are both forever in heart. You have been the evidence that love is real, it doesn't cost a thing, and one never has to jump through hoops to get it. I am so proud of the men you boys have grown up to be and continue to grow into being.

I love you both, worlds without end, infinity and beyond, and in all the spaces of my heart.

⊱ EVERYONE ELSE ⊰

The mention of your name on these pages should not be the only indicator of my gratitude or appreciation to have you in my life. Everything I have been through has been a part of my journey. You are a part of my journey, and although your name was not mentioned please know that you matter, I appreciate and thank you for being a part of my journey.

Additional Planners, Journals, Workbooks & More

- Surviving The Breakup and Preventing Others: Workbook and Journal
- Doing The Most Daily: Daily Tracker, Planner and Journal
- Gratitude and Wellness: Daily Tracker, Planner and Journal
- Mood and Habit: Daily Tracker, Planner and Journal
- Thoughts and Feelings: Daily Tracker, Planner and Journal

Poetry Books

- Poems from Love and Pain
- From My Heart and Rage to Yours
- From My Heart and Spirit to Yours
- From My Heart Rage and Spirit to Yours

Also Available

- Adults Coloring Books
- Mandala Coloring Books
- Motivational Coloring Books
- Affirmation Coloring Books
- Children Coloring Books
- Children Activities Books

TABLE OF CONTENT

ACKNOWLEDGMENTS …………………………………..2

INTRODUCTION ………………………………………......10

A GLIMPSE OF MY STORY………………………………12

GOALS AND AGREEMENT……….………………………17

JOURNAL GOALS AGREEMENT ………………………19

ABOUT ME ……………………………………………….20

LET ME CHECK ON ME ………………………………..26

HE SAID/SHE SAID ……………………………………..27

SNAPSHOT OF ME BEFORE MY EX …………………28

LAST THREE EXES ……………………………………..29

RELATIONSHIP TIME TABLE 1 ………………………32

RELATIONSHIP TIME TABLE 2 ………………………33

RELATIONSHIP TIME TABLE 3 ………………………34

HOW ARE YOU CURRENTLY FEELING AFTER YOUR REFLECTION? ………………………38

LET'S DIVE IN …………………………………………..39

N THE BEGINNING, THE MIDDLE, THE END ………40

IN THE BEGINNING ……………………………………. 41

PHYSICAL ATTRACTION………………………….…... 43

DESCRIBE YOUR FIRST DATE WITH THE FOLLOWING DETAILS ………………………………… 44

THE MIDDLE …………………………………………… 47

HOW WAS YOUR EX IN THE MIX? ………………… 53

THE JELLY IN THE MIDDLE …………………………. 57

LEARNING DYNAMICS ………………………….….... 63

FAMILY INTERACTION ……………………………… 65

MY EXES' MOTHER + FATHER 68
COMMONALITIES AND DIFFERENCES 69
THE FUNDAMENTALS....................................70
HE INTIMACY 71
SEX & INTIMACY 74
BACK IN BED 76
TAKE A MINUTE TO REVIEW AND PROCESS 80
THE END IN SIGHT 81
YESTERDAY 92
GOODBYE 94
AFFIRMATION 105
MOVING ON 106
AFFIRMATION 107
THE AFTERMATH AFTER THE BREAKUP 108
THE LAST TALK THAT NEVER HAPPENED 118
CRY IF YOU NEED TO CRY IF YOU NEED TO 121
FORGIVE THEM, FORGIVE YOURSELF, OVER
AND OVER AGAIN UNTIL THERE IS NOTHING
LEFT TO FORGIVE... 123
I WILL LEARN TO FORGIVE NOT FOR MY EX'S SAKE
BUT FOR MY FREEDOM 124
"WHAT FORGIVENESS IS NOT" PLEDGES 126
FORGIVENESS IS NOT ABOUT STAYING WITH
SOMEONE WHO IS TOXIC 127
HARSH REALITY REFLECTION 128
STAGES OF GRIEF 130

~ 7 ~

THIS TIME WAS SUPPOSED TO BE DIFFERENT
BUT WAS IT REALLY JUST THE SAME? 134

HUNTED……………………………………………… 135

MY POISON …………………………………………. 137

WOULD I KNOW IF MY RELATIONSHIP WAS
TOXIC? ………………………………………………….139

IT WASN'T JUST YOU ITS WAS ALSO ME SO NOW
WHAT? 149

CHAOS ………………………………………………….150

COMMUNICATION …………………………………153

THE TEACHER LECTURER …………………………...157

COMMUNICATION CHART …………………………158

WHEN YOU CAN NO LONGER RUN FROM THE
PAST, TURN AROUND AND FACE IT ……………… 162

THE HUNTING PAST …………………………………. 163

AM I READY FOR LOVE OR DO I JUST WANT TO BE
APPEASED? ………………………………………… 168

STRUGGLE PUZZLE …………………………………. 176

THIS IS ME …………………………………………. 179

THE PARTNER I PICKED ……………………………. 184

MY FUTURE PARTNER ……………………….. 191

CONJUNCTION JUNCTION WHAT'S YOU
FUNCTION? IS IT DYSFUNCTION…………………….198

FATHER'S DAY ……………………………………. 199

EXPECTATIONS TO MEET UNREALISTIC
STANDARDS ………………………………………….205

EXTREMELY CRITICAL ……………………………..205

SETTLED FOR UNMET NEEDS	206
POOR BOUNDARIES	206
WITHHOLD AFFECTION	207
PASSIVE AGGRESSIVENESS	207
DEPRESSION AND ANXIETY	208
UNABLE TO CONTROL TEMPER	208
ABUSIVE	209
NEGLECT	209
DISRESPECTFUL	210
MOCK, TALK DOWN TOM OR SHUT DOWN	210
SUBSTANCE ABUSE	211
DRAWN TO CHAOS, DRAMA, OR THEATRICS	211
PEOPLE PLEASING	212
MANIPULATION AND OR LIES	212
KNOWING THE HALF THE BATTLE	215
MOVING FORWARD THE TOP OF ONE MOUNTAIN IS THE BOTTOM OF ANOTHER	222
LET US MOVE FORWARD, NOW WHAT	224
NOW THAT I KNOW WHAT I WANT, HERE IS MY PROMISE TO MYSELF DEAR ME LETTE	233
WRAP UP	236

INTRODUCTION

I have succeeded brilliantly, failed drastically, crawled in and out of shame, bypassed and suppressed, acknowledged, and ignored, both pieces of and spaces within myself, all in the process of self-discovery. I am not a perfect example of a person who has 'made it' or has it all together. I am climbing up the mountain, and each summit is another mountain bottom. I am still learning every day along my journey.

This journey includes dating. At forty-five years old, I am single. I don't say that to insinuate that there is something wrong with being single; however, I believe that things would be different if I asked myself some of the questions in this workbook. If I took the time to consider some of the answers, I would have been more aware, perhaps made better choices and most importantly, identified and recognized things within myself that needed understanding, adjusting, cementing and exploring.

Until you know yourself, what you need and deserve, what areas you ought to maintain, improve, cling to or release, you will unlikely find a sustainable relationship or be ready when one finds you.

Adjusting perspectives, desires, expectations, limiting beliefs and narrowing scopes can open doors beyond you never imagined. We all want to find Mr. or Mrs. Right. However, the result could continue to be Mr. or Mrs. Ex if we do not learn to understand ourselves. Having full awareness of what we want or don't want, need or don't need, deserve or don't deserve, or our blind spots can help us to navigate more efficiently and authentically along our journey. Without this knowledge, we continue to settle for far too long in situations that should expire or hold on to things and or people who hurts us. We must decide that we can no longer make our choices for a partner based on fear or desperation.

I created this journal, and associated workbook course in order to help people dive beneath the epidermis of the issue and into the core of the matter. If you are ready to explore and examine yourself, your relationship, your breakup(s), your patterns, your cycles and, most importantly, your blind spots then let's do it. I promise that there will be a light at the end of the tunnel.

Are you ready? LET US BEGIN with your story.

In the following pages, you will find space for a brief biography with dots for you to fill in. Try not to think too hard about it. Let the answers flow naturally. Sometimes we are so far ahead, or in *over* our heads, that we forget to examine the ground we covered.

Start off with the basics, then tell allow yourself to recall the path you took while getting to where you are. Remind yourself of some of the pit stops and allow your body to let out any emotion that may feel uncomfortable as you process the prompts.

It may be a while since you thought about some of these questions. The answers may seem irrelevant to dating, but they are not. Each of these little elements play a role in the version of you that shows up in a relationship. The same questions, if answered about your partner, may affect the version of them that shows up in the relationship, too, without either of you knowing.

This brief exercise opens the conversation about your journey and some areas on which process or reflection may be needed. Any thoughts or concerns before we proceed?

……………………………………………………………………………………………..
……………………………………………………………………………………………..
……………………………………………………………………………………………..
……………………………………………………………………………………………..
……………………………………………………………………………………………..
……………………………………………………………………………………………..
……………………………………………………………………………………………..
……………………………………………………………………………………………..
……………………………………………………………………………………………..
……………………………………………………………………………………………..
……………………………………………………………………………………………..
……………………………………………………………………………………………..
……………………………………………………………………………………………..
……………………………………………………………………………………………..
……………………………………………………………………………………………..
……………………………………………………………………………………………..

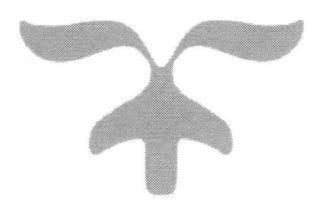

A GLIMPSE OF MY STORY

My name is ………………………………………..and I am ……………………
………………………………………………………………… I was born to a woman
who………………………………………………………………….and a man who
……………………………………………………………………………………..…

Before I was born my parents were

………………………………………………………………………………………….
………………………………………………………………………………………….
………………………………………………………………………………………….

and had plans to ……………………………………………………………………….

From what I know I was a planned/unplanned child, and this change my parents' life (how)

………………………………………………………………………………………….
………………………………………………………………………………………….
………………………………………………………………………………………….
………………………………………………………………………………………….
………………………………………………………………………………………….
………………………………………………………………………………………….

For the most part I would describe my parents as

………………………………………………………………………………………….
………………………………………………………………………………………….

and my family as

………………………………………………………………………………………….
………………………………………………………………………………………….
………………………………………………………………………………………….
………………………………………………………………………………………….

My childhood was ……………………………………………………………………………
……………………………………………………………………………………………………
……………………………………………………………………………………………………
……………………………………………………………………………………………………
with the exception of ………………………………………………………………………
……………………………………………………………………………………………………
……………………………………………………………………………………………………

Strong emotions I recall from childhood are……………………………………………
…………………………………………………………….. Strong emotions I've let go of from childhood are ………………………………………………………………………….
Strong emotions and issues I still hold on to, and struggle with at times, from childhood include……………………………………………………………………………………
……………………………………………………………………………………………………
……………………………………………………………………………………………………

As a teenager, I was ………………………………………………………………………
I remember feeling …………………………………………………………………………
often. This has caused me to struggle with…………………………………………………
………………………………………………………………… as a result. I have tried to be more ……………………………………………………………………………………………
because of what I have been through.

As much as I try, it's hard for me to
……………………………………………………………………………………………………
……………………………………….because memories of my teen years affect me
……………………………………………………………………………………………………
……………………………………………………………………………………………………

~ 14 ~

The experiences from young adulthood that have shaped or affected me includes ....
....
....
Which made me feel ....
Then and makes me feel .... now.

Overall, my family is, ... and I see myself as .... in my family. I am grateful for my .... because .... I resent my ....because ....
....
I have to numb or suppress my emotions when I am around ....
because..
....
which makes me feel ....

I forgive or have not forgiven ....
because..
....
....and
this affected me and continues to affect me
....

Socially speaking, I think I am .... Others may think I am .... but what they don't know is that I struggle with
....
....

~ 15 ~

My boundary system was ………………………………………… back then, and that has changed/stayed the same even today. Looking back at my life, I value ………………………………………. and regret ……………………………………… I have let go of ……………………………………………………. but still hold on/regret ………………………………………………………………………...

A significant action/trauma/event from my past that causes issues in my relationships is ………………………………………………………………………………………… Some of the impact of this has shown up in many ways in my relationships ………………………………………………………………………………………… ………………………………………………………………………………………… I realize that I need to work on ………………………………………… if I am to become ……………………………………………..failure to do so could result in …………………………………………………………………………………..

Change is ……………………...………………………………………. for me because ………………………………………………………………………………..………… But I know that…………………………….. …………………………………………... …………………………………………………………………………..……………… …………………………………………………………………………..…. I hope that ……………………………………………………………………………………

This is only a glimpse of my story, and the remaining chapters are still left up to ………………………………………………………………………………………… …………………………………………………………………………………………

GOALS AND AGREEMENT

Thank you for buying this Journal. It is my duty to ensure that your hard-earned money is well spent. This journal will help you one way or the other, I promise. That is my goal, and because you made the purchase, I would like to believe that is *our* goal. The first section of this book will identify your goals, and in the end, we will reflect to see if your goals were accomplished. Consider the following pledge, one that I encourage you to make for the work you'll do in this journal, and for the work you'll do in your life.

- I commit to doing the work necessary for my healing, growth, and development. This will enable me to make a better choice about the person I choose to be with.

- I understand that I cannot have whom I want or need if I do not know who I am. In order to choose the right person, I deserve from an authentic, healthy space, I commit to exploring the pages in this workbook in order to break a pattern that no longer serves me

☐ I agree
☐ I disagree
☐ Let's see

Signature: ……………………………………

Date: ……………………………………

Journal Goals Agreement

What do I want to get out of the process of exploring my breakups with this Journal:
……………………………………………………………………………………………
……………………………………………………………………………………………
……………………………………………………………………………………………
……………………………………………………………………………………………
………………………………………………How honest will you be on a scale of 1-10?

1☐   2☐   3☐   4☐   5☐   6☐   7☐   8☐   9☐   10☐

I will know that I'm being honest because……………………………………………
……………………………………………………………………………………………
……………………………………………………………………………………………

This process is important to me and for me because ……………………………
……………………………………………………………………………………………
……………………………………………………………………………………………
……………………………………………………………………………………………

Notes :
……………………………………………………………………………………………
……………………………………………………………………………………………
……………………………………………………………………………………………
……………………………………………………………………………………………
……………………………………………………………………………………………
……………………………………………………………………………………………

ABOUT ME

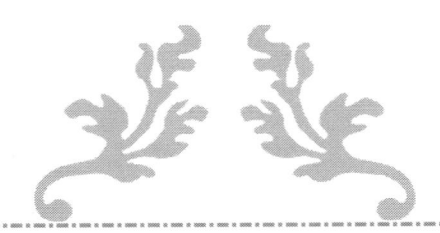

ABOUT ME

Who am I?

....
....
....
....

Who do I think I am?

....
....
....
....

Who do I want to be?

....
....
....
....

Why do I want to be who I am? Or am I trying to be something else?

....
....
....
....

If so, why do I want to be whom I am trying to be?

....
....
....
....

What do I think is wrong with who I am?

....
....
....
....

Am I trying to change?

....
....
....
....

Is who I am tied to the things I value?

....
....
....
....

Is who I am perceived to be what I value?

....
....
....
....

Who do I bring to my relationships?

....
....
....
....

What do I bring to my relationships?

....
....
....
....

Who am I on the inside?

....
....
....
....

Who am I not on the outside?

....
....
....
....

Where does my happiness come from?

....
....
....
....

Is my happiness inside, or do I look outside for it?

....
....
....
....

What do I run to?

....
....
....
....

What do I run from?

....
....
....
....

How has my growing up impacted me?

....
....
....
....

Am I healed, healing, or wounded?

....
....
....
....

LET ME CHECK ON ME

HE SAID, SHE SAID

SNAPSHOT BEFORE MY EX

LAST THREE EXES

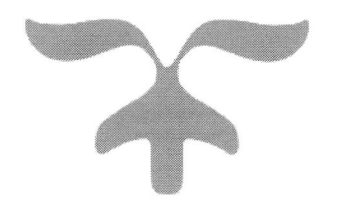

❧ *LET ME CHECK ON ME* ☙

Check all that apply

Right Now

☐ My last relationship ended
☐ I am thinking about ending my current relationship
☐ I am in a situation that is complicated
☐ I am waiting
☐ I broke up with my ex
☐ My ex broke up with me

Relationship status after breakup:

☐ Divorced
☐ Single
☐ Moved on
☐ Waiting

MOOD

Mood at break up: 😀 😆 🙁 😟 😣 😇 🙂 😌 😁 😱 😩

Mood right after: 😀 😆 🙁 😟 😣 😇 🙂 😌 😁 😱 😩

Current mood: 😀 😆 🙁 😟 😣 😇 🙂 😌 😁 😱 😩

Notes:

Mood at break up

....
....

Mood right after

....
....

Current mood

....
....

HE SAID /SHE SAID

How long was your last relationship?

....

....

When did it end? ....

How long ago was that? ....

What was the given reason FOR THE BREAKUP, according to your ex?

....

....

....

What do you think was the reason?

....

....

....

What is the difference between the two reasons?

....

....

....

....

....

....

....

❦ *SNAPSHOT OF ME BEFORE MY EX* ❦

I was: ……………………………………………………………………………………………..

………………………………………………………………..……………………………………

……………………………………………………………………………………………………..

……………………………………………………………………………………………………..

My social life included:

………………………………………………………………………………………..……………

……………………………………………………………………………………………………..

……………………………………………………………………………………………………..

……………………………………………………………………………………………………..

My typical day was………………………………………………………………………………….

……………………………………………………………………………………………………..

……………………………………………………………………..……………………………….

……………………………………………………………………………………………………..

My goals included …………………………………………………………………..……………..

……………………………………………………………………..……………………………….

……………………………………………………………………………………………………..

……………………………………………………………………………………………………..

My priorities were …………………………………………………………………………………..

……………………………………………………………………………………………………..

…………………………………………………………………..…………………………………..

……………………………………………………………………………………………………..

……………………………………………………………………………………………………..

~ 28 ~

LAST THREE EXES

The following questions pertain to your past three relationships

My dating mindset before my 1st Ex was:
- ☐ I'm looking.
- ☐ Either way I'm good
- ☐ I really need to find someone
- ☐ I am running out of time
- ☐ I'm lonely
- ☐ I don't want to get into a relationship
- ☐ Other _____

My dating mindset before (2 Ex ago) was:
- ☐ I'm looking
- ☐ Either way I'm good
- ☐ I really need to find someone
- ☐ I am running out of time
- ☐ I'm lonely
- ☐ I don't want to get into a relationship
- ☐ Other _____

My dating mindset before (3 Ex ago) was:
- ☐ I'm looking
- ☐ Either way I'm good
- ☐ I really need to find someone
- ☐ I am running out of time
- ☐ I'm lonely
- ☐ I don't want to get into a relationship
- ☐ Other _____

What were your reasons for that attitude or choice?

In your responses, it is important to examine what your mindset was before each of your last three relationships. Did you change your mindset to make room for any of the relationships? Are there patterns that you recognize? Why were you in the mental space that you were in prior to each relationship? Were there any significant events that played a role in any of these mindsets?

1st Ex :

....
....
....

2nd Ex :

....
....
....

3rd Ex :

....
....
....

NOTES OR REFLECTIONS:

....
....
....
....
....
....

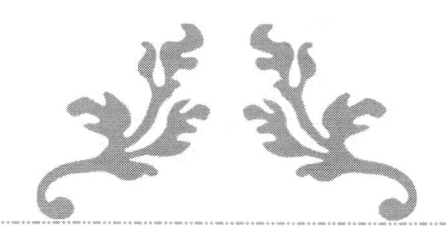

RELATIONSHIP TIME TABLE 1

RELATIONSHIP TIME TABLE 2

RELATIONSHIP TIME TABLE 3

❧ Relationship Time table 1 ❧

Use the table below to complete the information about your last four relationships. If the number is less than four, use what applies.

1. In the first column, list the name or initials.
2. In the second column, list when you met (month or season).
3. In the third column, list when you broke up (month or season).
4. In the fourth column, list how long the relationship lasted (month or season).
5. In the last column, use one word that defines why you broke up.

NAME	MET	BROKE UP	DURATION	NOTE

❧ Relationship Timetable 2 ☙

Using the table below, rate on a scale of 1-10 (10 being the best), the traits of the last four relationships you've been in. If the number is less than four, use what applies.

1. In the first column, list the name or initials.
2. In the second column, assign a number for how well your partner provided what you needed.
3. In the third column, assign a number for how well your partner provided what you wanted.
4. In the fourth column, provide a rating for how patient your partner was with you.
5. In the fifth column, provide a rating for how stable you viewed yourself.
6. In the sixth column, provide a rating for how kind you viewed your partner.
7. In the sixth column, provide a rating for how sexually compatible your partner was.

NAME	WHAT I NEEDED	WHAT I WANTED	PATIENCE	STABILITY	KINDNESS	SEX

❧ *Relationship Time Table 3* ❦

Using the table, check the box that best describes what you feel in your heart, not your brain (this is where the honestly pledge is extremely important). Consider how you feel about your last 4 relationships.

1. If the number is less than four, use what applies.
2. If you feel like you have no unresolved feelings, check the box marked resolved.
3. If you feel like you have partially resolved feelings, check partially.
4. If you feel like you have unresolved feelings, check unresolved.
5. If it is complicated, check complicated.

NAME	RESOLVED	PARTIALLY	UNRESOLVED	COMPLICATED

Take a break and review each chart then state your observations below

Table 1: I notice/realize/reminded myself/that:

....
....
....
....
....
....

Table 2: I notice/realize/reminded myself/ that:

....
....
....
....
....
....

Table 3: I notice/realize/reminded myself/ that:

....
....
....
....
....
....

BELOW, MAKE A NOTE ABOUT STRONG SIMILARITIES OR DIFFERENCES

....
....
....
....
....
....

Have you been

As you completed the tables, you took a small trip back down memory lane. How far did you have to go to access those memories about your past relationships?

Were they closer to the surface than you thought, or were they right where you expected?

Was there anything that surprised you? What and why did it?

Take a few minutes to think about it.

Did you feel the same emotion or energy moving through you when you thought about all your exes? Did you have the same feelings as you thought about each of them?

....
....
....

Did you feel yourself dealing with the same issues with all the exes or most of them?

....
....

Did you feel distinct differences or similarities in your choices?

....
....

Were your choices getting better or were they getting worse (by your standard)?

....
....

What are some things your observations might reveal to you?

....
....

What are you resisting as you think about your observations?

....
....

Additional Notes:

....
....

How are you currently feeling after your reflection?

Check all that apply?

☐ Sadness
☐ Anger
☐ Guilt
☐ Rejected
☐ Confusion
☐ Loneliness
☐ Similar and opposite words
☐ Heartbroken
☐ Suffering disappointment
☐ Overwhelmed
☐ Distress upset
☐ Anguished
☐ Violated
☐ Betrayed
☐ Abandoned
☐ Hurt
☐ Displaced
☐ Closed off
☐ Shut down
☐ Devastated
☐ Broken-hearted
☐ Heavy-hearted
☐ Suffering
☐ Grieving
☐ Grief-stricken
☐ Inconsolable
☐ Crushed
☐ Shattered
☐ OTHER WRITE BELOW

…………………………………………

…………………………………………

…………………………………………

…………………………………………

❦ *Let's Dive In* ❦

The previous section examined a snapshot of some of your past relationships. Hopefully, that revisit allowed you to see a picture. Now let us go in a little closer and examine some more targeted moments. In the next section, we will focus on your last relationship, starting from the beginning.

Try to take the perspective of the observer instead of the person re-experiencing all the emotions; the good, bad, and ugly. Don't run from what you feel but don't sit in the old emotions too long.

It is possible that you may feel some element of grief as you go down memory lane but don't be tempted to ruminate, even if it feels comfortable. Imagine that you are a witness, and you also have the inside track of what happened, so you have an advantage.

As we re-examine this relationship closely, we will look at the strands, blind spots, bypasses, and compromise made with or without knowing.

If the memory is too overwhelming, take a step back and come back when you are ready.

Are you ready? Ok, let's talk about your last relationship.

As we recall, not rewrite the story of us, let us start from the beginning with this **trajectory timeline.**

Deep Breathe in, Deep Breath out.
Deep Breathe in, Deep Breath out.
Deep Breathe in, Deep Breath out.
Deep Breathe in, Deep Breath out.
Deep Breathe in, Deep Breath out.
Deep Breathe in, Deep Breath out.
Deep Breathe in, Deep Breath out.
Deep Breathe in, Deep Breath out.
Deep Breathe in, Deep Breath out.
Deep Breathe in, Deep Breath out.
Deep Breathe in, Deep Breath out.
Deep Breathe in, Deep Breath out.
Deep Breathe in, Deep Breath out.
Deep Breathe in, Deep Breath out.

IN THE BEGINNING, THE MIDDLE, THE END

IN THE BEGINNING

My ex could be described with this one word: ……………………………………………..…..

When did you meet? :……………………………………………………………………………..

Where did you meet? ……………………………………………………………………..……...

What was your mood at your first encounter? ……………………………………………...…………..

What was your ex-mood at your first encounter? ………………………………………….……..

Have you ever asked your ex what was their first impression of you? ………………..……..

If so, what was it? ………………………………………………………………………………….

What was your first impression of them? ……………………………………………………….

What was the chemistry at that INSTANCE? ……………………………………………………

What was the connection? ………………………………………………………………………...

What did you find attractive about them? ……………………………………………………...

What did they find attractive about you? ……………………………………………………….

How comfortable did you feel? ……………………………………………………………….…..

Who FIRST asked for a telephone number or contact details?
……

How long did the first meeting/conversation last? …………………………………...………..

What did it feel like? What emotions did it evoke? ………………………………...…………..

Did you know for sure you wanted to see or talk again or were you indifferent, unimpressed or something else? why? ……………………………………………………………………
…………………………………………………………………………………………………
…………………………………………………………………………………………………
…………………………………………………………………………………………………

Who made the first move? ………………………………………………………………
…………………………………………………………………………………………………

Describe it:

…………………………………………………………………………………………………
…………………………………………………………………………………………………
…………………………………………………………………………………………………
…………………………………………………………………………………………………
…………………………………………………………………………………………………
…………………………………………………………………………………………………
…………………………………………………………………………………………………
…………………………………………………………………………………………………
…………………………………………………………………………………………………
…………………………………………………………………………………………………
…………………………………………………………………………………………………

❦ *Physical Attraction* ❧

On your personal scale of physical attraction, how would you rate your ex?

1☐ 2☐ 3☐ 4☐ 5☐ 6☐ 7☐ 8☐ 9☐ 10☐

Was there something physically about them that you were not attracted to?
....

What made you see past that?
....

What physical attributes did you find the most attractive?
....

What physical attributes did you find the least attractive?
....

What physical attributes did they find the least attractive about you?
....

What physical attributes did they find the most attractive about you?
....

How much of your attraction do you think was superficial?
....

How much of their attraction do you think was superficial?
....

How was this similar or different from your first encounter with your ex before this ex?
....
....
....
....
....
....
....
....

Describe your first date with the following details:

Who asked who out? ....

Was the feel of the date romantic/matter of fact/ formal/comfortable? ....

Where did you go on your first date? ....

Who planned it? ....

Did he or she dress appropriately or with effort? ....

Did you dress appropriately or with effort? ....

What did you notice that you hadn't before? ....

What did you notice from that first date that stayed consistent throughout the relationship?

....

....

....

Was there something that made you uncomfortable? ....

Was there something that made you feel at home? ....

On the date, did you find yourself comparing them to anyone? ....

....

What did you like or love about the date? ....

....

....

~ 44 ~

Was there anything you noticed, didn't focus on too much but made a mental note?
....
....

Who paid for the date? ....

How would you compare this first date in comparison to the previous first date of your relationship prior? (Better/Worse/More or Less fun/More or Less intense)
....
....
....
....
....

Was there oversharing? Oversharing is one person telling the other intimate details about relationships, friendships, family matters, or personal drama.

If so, on whose part? In other words, did either of you tell each other your whole life story?
....
....

Did they remind you of anyone? Family/Friend/Ex ....
....
....

Was there any promise you made to yourself prior to this date that you kept or broke?
....
....
....

I walked away from the first date feeling like ....

We ended up hooking up after the first date and I felt as a result (answer if this applies)

....

....

....

If so, looking back now, how do you feel about that decision

....

....

Overall, I would describe the first date as ....

....

....

....

....

....

....

....

....

....

....

....

‌ THE MIDDLE ‌

How long did you date before the relationship became exclusive? ………...……………..….

If not exclusive, what were the circumstances around that?

………………………………………………………………………………………………

………………………………………………………..……………………………………..

Whose idea was exclusivity? ………………………………………………………..……..

Was there pushback, resistance, or mutual agreement? …………………………………..

Were there already issues or concerns in the transition from dating to relationship phase?

If so, explain………………………………………………………………………………….

………………………………………………………………………………………………

………………………………………………………..……………………………………..

………………………………………………………………………………………………

Was the transition:
- ☐ Natural- with time
- ☐ Organic mutually agreed
- ☐ Negotiated- several discussions
- ☐ Forced- one person asking why not
- ☐ Rushed- very fast
- ☐ Lock down- fear of a FOMO

Looking back, was the transition too fast? ……………………………………………..…..

Why or Why Not?

………………………………………………………………………………………………

………………………………………………………..……………………………………..

………………………………………………………………………………………………

THE MIDDLE

Make a note about any significant event or incident that took place during the phase of transitioning from dating to relationship.

....
....
....
....
....
....

It is important to reflect on the flow of the relationship and how it transitioned from the dating stage to exclusivity. Were there several discussions that took place? Did you have to convince your ex, or did they have to convince you? Did the transition feel force or natural?

....
....
....
....
....
....
....
....
....
....
....
....

How Was Your Ex in the Mix?

Did your ex show kindness to people they interacted with? Such as waiter/ strangers/ family/ friends etc………………………………..……...…..………………………………………..…..

Was your ex frequently condescending or sarcastic? ………………………………………..

Were most of the stories they told about them? ………………………………………………

Did their stories always include them being cool, saying the right thing, having a snappy come back etc.? ………………………………………………………………………………...

Did your ex blame you or others for things instead of taking responsibility when an issue came up? ……………………………………………………………………………..………

Did your ex exhibit hostile or passive aggressive behavior? ………………………………….

Was your ex dishonest? …………………………………………………………...…………

Was your ex disrespectful to others? ……………………………………………….…..……

Was your ex overly independent? …………………………………………..……..…………

Was your ex too dependent or needy?…………………………………………..……………

Did your ex make you feel bad when you expressed your feelings?…………………….……
…………………………………………………………………………………………..

Did you limit yourself from sharing your feelings because they took things personally? ……………………………………………………………………………………………
……………………………………………………………………..……………………
………………………………………………………………………………………………

How Was Your Ex in the Mix?

Did you feel tense when you were around them?	☐Yes	☐No	☐Unsure
Was there any tension early in the relationship?	☐Yes	☐No	☐Unsure
Did your ex make you feel guilty a lot?	☐Yes	☐No	☐Unsure
Did your ex have healthy relationships with peers, family and coworkers?	☐Yes	☐No	☐Unsure
Did your ex apologize when needed?	☐Yes	☐No	☐Unsure
Did your ex seem unhappy to be alone?	☐Yes	☐No	☐Unsure
Did your ex feel like you were rescuing them?	☐Yes	☐No	☐Unsure
Did your ex feel like they were rescuing you?	☐Yes	☐No	☐Unsure
Did your ex avoid conflicts and confrontations?	☐Yes	☐No	☐Unsure
Did your ex exhibit passive aggressive behaviors?	☐Yes	☐No	☐Unsure
Did your ex cut off old friendships?	☐Yes	☐No	☐Unsure
Did your ex expect you to cut off old friendships?	☐Yes	☐No	☐Unsure
Did your ex have unresolved past relationships?	☐Yes	☐No	☐Unsure
Did your ex have unresolved current relationships?	☐Yes	☐No	☐Unsure
Did your ex show genuine interest in your kids?	☐Yes	☐No	☐Unsure
Was your ex overly involved in family matters?	☐Yes	☐No	☐Unsure
Did your ex respect your boundaries?	☐Yes	☐No	☐Unsure
Did your ex respect others' boundaries?	☐Yes	☐No	☐Unsure
Did your ex have bullying tendencies?	☐Yes	☐No	☐Unsure
Did your ex make you feel good at times?	☐Yes	☐No	☐Unsure
Did the relationship make you feel anxious?	☐Yes	☐No	☐Unsure
Did you feel like you were settling?	☐Yes	☐No	☐Unsure
Was your ex inconsistent?	☐Yes	☐No	☐Unsure
Did your ex tell you how to dress or to act?	☐Yes	☐No	☐Unsure
Did your ex break your physical boundaries with unwanted physical touch, even rubs or pokes when you asked them not to?	☐Yes	☐No	☐Unsure

How Was Your Ex in the Mix?

Cheek grabbing, hugs when you've indicated "not now"	☐Yes	☐No	☐Unsure
Did your ex roll their eyes at you a lot?	☐Yes	☐No	☐Unsure
Was your ex cruel to their parents?	☐Yes	☐No	☐Unsure
Was your ex secretive about little things?	☐Yes	☐No	☐Unsure
Was your ex secretive about big things?	☐Yes	☐No	☐Unsure
Did your ex need constant assurance?	☐Yes	☐No	☐Unsure
Did your ex employ double standards?	☐Yes	☐No	☐Unsure
Did your ex require constant contact?	☐Yes	☐No	☐Unsure
Did your ex exhibit jealous behavior?	☐Yes	☐No	☐Unsure
Were you pressured for an early commitment?	☐Yes	☐No	☐Unsure
Did your ex blame others for everything?	☐Yes	☐No	☐Unsure
Did your ex shut down frequently?	☐Yes	☐No	☐Unsure
Did your ex often have road rage?	☐Yes	☐No	☐Unsure
Was your ex overly friendly and sought approval?	☐Yes	☐No	☐Unsure
Did your ex show up unannounced or uninvited?	☐Yes	☐No	☐Unsure
Did your ex show signs of always having to be right?	☐Yes	☐No	☐Unsure
Did your ex take more than they gave?	☐Yes	☐No	☐Unsure
Was your ex clingy?	☐Yes	☐No	☐Unsure
Did your ex support your dreams?	☐Yes	☐No	☐Unsure
Did they ask a lot about you?	☐Yes	☐No	☐Unsure
Did your ex have a temper?	☐Yes	☐No	☐Unsure
Did your ex have a weird attitude?	☐Yes	☐No	☐Unsure
Did their social media account have rants/rage/ inappropriate or disrespectful posts about others?	☐Yes	☐No	☐Unsure
Was your ex unable to take criticism?	☐Yes	☐No	☐Unsure
Was your ex dismissive of your feelings?	☐Yes	☐No	☐Unsure

How Was Your Ex in the Mix?

Your ex had an unpleasant body odor.	☐Yes	☐No	☐Unsure
Your ex likes sex more than you did at the time.	☐Yes	☐No	☐Unsure
Your ex's anxiety made you anxious.	☐Yes	☐No	☐Unsure
You were embarrassed to introduce them to your family and friends.	☐Yes	☐No	☐Unsure
Your instincts said you should flee.	☐Yes	☐No	☐Unsure
Your friends and family didn't like them.	☐Yes	☐No	☐Unsure
Your ex never complimented you.	☐Yes	☐No	☐Unsure
They never responded or showed empathy even when you were upset.	☐Yes	☐No	☐Unsure
They had to dig deep to find emotion.	☐Yes	☐No	☐Unsure
Your ex thought and talked more of themselves than you.	☐Yes	☐No	☐Unsure
Did your ex often say "get over it"?	☐Yes	☐No	☐Unsure
Did it feel like they were playing games with a gas lighter?	☐Yes	☐No	☐Unsure

How were you in the mix?

Did you show kindness to people you interacted with including waiters/ strangers/ family/ friends?

....

....

Were you frequently condescending or sarcastic? ....

Were most of the stories about you? ....

Did your stories always include being cool, saying the right thing, having a snappy come back etc.? ....

Did you blame them or others for things instead of taking responsibility when an issue came up? ....

Did you exhibit hostile or passive aggressive behavior? ....

Were you dishonest? ....

Were you disrespectful to others? ....

Were you overly independent? ....

Were you dependent or needy? ....

Did you make them feel bad when they expressed their feelings? ....

....

Did they limit themselves from sharing their feelings because you took things personally?

....

How were you in the mix?

Did they feel tense when they were around you?	☐Yes	☐No	☐Unsure
Was there tension early in the relationship?	☐Yes	☐No	☐Unsure
Did you ever guilt trip them?	☐Yes	☐No	☐Unsure
Did you have healthy relationships with peers, family and coworkers?	☐Yes	☐No	☐Unsure
Did you apologize when needed?	☐Yes	☐No	☐Unsure
Did you seem unhappy to be alone?	☐Yes	☐No	☐Unsure
Did they feel like they were rescuing you?	☐Yes	☐No	☐Unsure
Did you avoid conflicts and confrontations?	☐Yes	☐No	☐Unsure
Did you exhibit passive aggressive behaviors?	☐Yes	☐No	☐Unsure
Did you cut off old friendships?	☐Yes	☐No	☐Unsure
Did you expect them to cut off old friendships?	☐Yes	☐No	☐Unsure
Did you have unresolved past relationships?	☐Yes	☐No	☐Unsure
Did you show genuine interest in their kids?	☐Yes	☐No	☐Unsure
Were you overly involved in family matters?	☐Yes	☐No	☐Unsure
Did you respect their boundaries?	☐Yes	☐No	☐Unsure
Did you have bullying tendencies?	☐Yes	☐No	☐Unsure
Did the relationship make them feel good?	☐Yes	☐No	☐Unsure
Did the relationship make them feel anxious?	☐Yes	☐No	☐Unsure
Did you feel like they were settling?	☐Yes	☐No	☐Unsure
Were you inconsistent?	☐Yes	☐No	☐Unsure
Did you tell them how to dress or to act?	☐Yes	☐No	☐Unsure
Did you break their physical boundaries? Ex: rubs, poking, etc.	☐Yes	☐No	☐Unsure
Any cheek grabbing, hugs when they indicated "not now"?	☐Yes	☐No	☐Unsure
Did you roll your eyes at them a lot?	☐Yes	☐No	☐Unsure

How were you in the mix?

Were you cruel to their parents?	☐Yes	☐No	☐Unsure
Were you secretive about little things?	☐Yes	☐No	☐Unsure
Were you secretive about big things?	☐Yes	☐No	☐Unsure
Did you need constant assurance?	☐Yes	☐No	☐Unsure
Did you uphold any double standards?	☐Yes	☐No	☐Unsure
Did you require constant contact?	☐Yes	☐No	☐Unsure
Did you exhibit jealous behavior?	☐Yes	☐No	☐Unsure
Did you pressure them for an early commitment?	☐Yes	☐No	☐Unsure
Did you blame others instead of taking responsibility?	☐Yes	☐No	☐Unsure
Did you shut down frequently?	☐Yes	☐No	☐Unsure
Did they often have road rage?	☐Yes	☐No	☐Unsure
Were they overly friendly and sought approval?	☐Yes	☐No	☐Unsure
Did they show up unannounced or uninvited?	☐Yes	☐No	☐Unsure
Did you show signs of always being right?	☐Yes	☐No	☐Unsure
Did you take more than they gave?	☐Yes	☐No	☐Unsure
Were you clingy?	☐Yes	☐No	☐Unsure
Did you support their dreams?	☐Yes	☐No	☐Unsure
Did you ask a lot about them?	☐Yes	☐No	☐Unsure
Did you have a temper?	☐Yes	☐No	☐Unsure
Did you have a crazy friend?	☐Yes	☐No	☐Unsure
Did your social media account have rants/rage/ inappropriate or disrespectful posts about others?	☐Yes	☐No	☐Unsure
Were you unable to take criticism?	☐Yes	☐No	☐Unsure
Were you dismissive of your feelings?	☐Yes	☐No	☐Unsure
I had an unpleasant body odor.	☐Yes	☐No	☐Unsure
Did you like the sex more than they did?	☐Yes	☐No	☐Unsure
Your anxiety made you anxious.	☐Yes	☐No	☐Unsure

How were you in the mix?

They were embarrassed to introduce you to their family and friends.	☐Yes	☐No	☐Unsure
They had impulses to flee.	☐Yes	☐No	☐Unsure
Did their friends and family like you?	☐Yes	☐No	☐Unsure
Did you ever compliment them?	☐Yes	☐No	☐Unsure
Did you respond or show empathy even when they were upset?	☐Yes	☐No	☐Unsure
Did you have to dig deep to find emotion?	☐Yes	☐No	☐Unsure
Did you think and talk more about yourself than them?	☐Yes	☐No	☐Unsure
Did you often say "get over it"?	☐Yes	☐No	☐Unsure
Did it feel like you were playing games with them?	☐Yes	☐No	☐Unsure
Did you gas light?	☐Yes	☐No	☐Unsure

🕿 *The Jelly in the Middle* 🕿

What were the areas of your relationship that worked well?

....
....
....
....

What were the areas of your relationship that did not work well?

....
....
....
....

When did you start to notice changes?

....
....
....
....

Were they slow, gradual, or quick?

....
....
....
....

❧ *The Jelly in the Middle* ❦

How much time did you spend together on average?

....
....
....
....

Did you move to be with them, or did they move to be with you?

....
....
....
....

If you moved in with each other how long was the relationship going before the move-in together?

....
....
....
....

In retrospect, was it too soon?

....
....
....
....

🌺 *The Jelly in the Middle* 🌺

How often did you regret being in the relationship?

....

....

Did you feel like you had a partner?

....

....

How often did you go on dates?

....

....

Who took the initiative?

....

....

Describe how the relationship met your expectations.

....

....

Who was more affectionate?

....

....

Describe how the relationship failed any of your expectations.

....

....

🙢 *The Jelly in the Middle* 🙠

How happy would you say you were in the relationship?

....

....

Was there a friendship in your relationship?

....

....

How well did your Ex meet your needs?

....

....

How much did you trust your ex?

....

....

....

How much did your Ex trust you?

....

....

....

How rewarding was your relationship with your ex?

....

....

....

❧ *The Jelly in the Middle* ☙

How happy would you say your ex was in the relationship?

....
....
....

When you looked at your ex, you **felt** like:

....
....
....

When you think about your ex, you **feel** like:

....
....
....
....
....
....
....
....
....
....
....
....
....
....

Answer the questions below True of False

I think that my ex loved me.	☐T	☐F
My ex-maintained eye contact during conversations.	☐T	☐F
My ex was very affectionate.	☐T	☐F
My ex frequently interrupted when I tried to explain.	☐T	☐F
My ex paid enough attention to me.	☐T	☐F
I paid enough attention to my ex.	☐T	☐F
My ex complimented me a lot.	☐T	☐F
My ex skipped important arguments.	☐T	☐F
I remembered special occasions or anniversaries?	☐T	☐F
I was excited about the relationship?	☐T	☐F
I was disappointed you about the relationship?	☐T	☐F
This relationship was different from my previous relationships.	☐T	☐F
I could tell the difference between their thoughts and their feelings?	☐T	☐F
I could tell the difference between my thoughts and my feelings?	☐T	☐F
I was able to see things from their point of view easily?	☐T	☐F
Were they able to see things from my point of view?	☐T	☐F
My ex maintained eye contact during conversations.	☐T	☐F
My ex was very affectionate.	☐T	☐F
My ex frequently interrupted when I tried to explain.	☐T	☐F
My ex paid enough attention to me.	☐T	☐F
I paid enough attention to my ex.	☐T	☐F
My ex always complimented me	☐T	☐F
My ex skipped important arguments.	☐T	☐F

❧ Learning Dynamics ❧

Communication	Rarely	Often	Never
Did you ever feel like they were putting words in your mouth?			
Did you feel misunderstood by your ex?			
Did you find it hard to communicate?			
Did you find it easy to communicate?			
Did they make assumptions about what you were about to say?			
Did you make assumptions about what they were about to say?			
Were they attentive when you spoke?			
Were you attentive when they spoke?			
Did you feel like your point of view got across?			
Did they feel like their point of view got across?			
Did they have a "tone" when you spoke?			
Did they interrupt you when you spoke?			
Did you interrupt when they spoke?			
Did you clarify or summarize after you spoke?			
Did they clarify or summarize after they spoke?			
Did they gaze off when you spoke or appear uninterested?			
Did they pay attention to facts only when you spoke and ignored the emotional tone?			
Did they attempt to finish your sentence or thoughts?			
Did you bite your tongue?			
Did they get angry when you disagreed?			

Communication	Rarely	Often	Never
Did they often change the subject when it wasn't about them?			
Did they listen attentively?			
Were they critical?			
Were they condescending?			
Were they sarcastic?			
My ex kept scores.			
My ex threw things at my face often.			
My ex lied to me.			
Did they take ownership of issues?			
Did they look for compromises?			
Did they shut down?			
Did they walk away or out during conflicts or misunderstandings?			
Did they ask for help?			
Did they seem like they were thinking about what to say next instead of listening?			

❧ *Family Interaction* ❧

My ex's relationship with my kids was (if applicable):

....
....
....

My ex's relationship with my family was:

....
....
....

My ex's relationship with their kids was (if applicable):

....
....
....

My ex's relationship with their family was:

....
....
....

What I liked about their interaction with their family was:

....
....
....

❧ Family Interaction ❧

What I did not like about their interaction with their family was:

....
....
....

What I did not like about their interaction with my family was:

....
....
....

What I liked about their interaction with my family was:

....
....
....
....
....
....

What I did not like about their family was:

....
....
....
....
....
....

HOW FAR DOES THE APPLE FALL FROM THE TREE?

❦ *MY EXES' Mother + Father* ❦

The relationship my ex had with their parents was healthy.	☐T	☐F
The relationship my ex had with their mother was healthy.	☐T	☐F
The relationship my ex had with their father was healthy.	☐T	☐F
My ex was punishing to their parents.	☐T	☐F
My ex was punishing to their mom.	☐T	☐F
My ex was punishing to their dad.	☐T	☐F

REFLECTIONS:

....
....
....
....
....
....
....
....
....
....
....
....
....
....
....
....

Commonalities and Differences

Complete the chart below by checking the appropriate box that describes the commonalities you shared with your ex about these fundamental opinions/values below. On the left is the category on the right is a comparison.

The Basics	Different	Similar	Opposite
Core Values			
Family Values			
Family Tradition			
Work Ethic			
Views on making a relationship public			
Long term goals			
Short term goals			
Career goals			
Views on who pays for the bills			
Gambling			
Recreation			
Drugs			
Self-care			
Reassurance requirement			

REFLECTIONS:

....
....
....
....
....
....

🙟 The Fundamentals 🙞

Our physical attraction can be animalistic in the grand scheme of things. Passion can sometimes blind us to even the most obvious things. Consider the areas listed in the table in the chart below, and then decide whether you and your ex shared similar, opposing, or similar views in each of these areas.

Action	Similar	Opposite	Same
Attitude towards facing challenges			
Spiritual path			
Communication			
Conflict resolution			
Finances			
Budgeting			
Religion			
Political			

Reflection: ……………………………………………………………………………………
……………………………………………………………………………………………………
……………………………………………………………………………………………………
……………………………………………………………………………………………………
……………………………………………………………………………………………………

❧ *The Intimacy* ❦

"Let's talk about sex, baby, let's talk about you and me, let's talk about all the good things, and the bad things that may be"
Salt, Pepa & Spinderella

My idea of a romantic evening is

....
....
....
....

How often did I have this with my ex?

....
....
....
....

The most satisfying sexual encounters included

....
....
....
....

I did or did not experience satisfying sexual encounters frequently with my ex

....
....
....

The Intimacy

I initiate sexual intimacy by

....
....
....
....

My ex initiated sexual encounters by

....
....
....
....

I initiate emotional intimacy by

....
....
....
....

My ex initiated emotional intimacy by

....
....
....
....

I initiate physical intimacy by

....
....
....
....

The Intimacy

My ex initiated physical intimacy by

....
....
....

I wanted my ex to do more

....
....

My ex wanted me to do more or be more -------- sexually

....
....

I wish I was able to .... with my ex

....
....
....
....

I wanted to explore more sexually with my ex

....
....
....
....

My ex wanted to explore more -------- sexually with me

....
....
....
....

Sex & Intimacy

In the chart below, select the commonalities or differences for the action items below. Place a check box in the area that best describes the similarities and differences in your relationship.

Action	Similar	Middle	Different
Love language			
Sex Drive			
Sexual compatibility			
Physical desire for each other			
Emotional Intimacy			
Traditional experimental			
Mutual Satisfaction During Intimacy			
Catering			

What did you realize and how do you feel about it? ....
....
....
....
....

❧ *Back in Bed* ❦

How would you describe the first intimate encounter with your ex? ………………………..

………………………………………………………………………………………………

………………………………………………………………………………………………

………………………………………………………………………………………………

………………………………………………………………………………………………

How did it change over time? …………………………………………………..………..

………………………………………………………………………………………………

………………………………………………………………………………………………

………………………………………………………………………………………………

………………………………………………………………………………………………

Most of the time, the sex between us felt like: …………………………..……………......

………………………………………………………………………………………………

………………………………………………………………………………………………

………………………………………………………………………………………………

Was there a change in intimacy? If so when and why?

………………………………………………………………………………………..……

………………………………………………………………………………………..……

………………………………………………………………………………………...……

Were you connected during intimacy?

………………………………………………………………………………………………

………………………………………………………………………………………………

………………………………………………………………………………………………

………………………………………………………………………………………………

~ 75 ~

❧ *Back in Bed* ❧

Were you disconnected during intimacy?

....

....

....

....

Did you feel safe? ....

Did you feel sexy? ....

Did you feel wanted? ....

Did you feel satisfied? ....

Did your mind often wander during sex? ....

Did this happen with your ex more than others?

....

Who initiated intimacy more, you or your ex?

....

Was there foreplay? ....

How did you feel about the foreplay? ....

Was the level of affection what you wanted? ....

Was the emotional connection strong or lacking? ....

❧ *Back in Bed* ❦

Was there anything you like that your partner didn't do sexually?

....

....

....

If the answer to the previous question is yes, did you ever vocalize it? ....

....

Did your partner(s) orgasm or ejaculate prematurely? ....

If the answer to the previous question was yes, how frequently did this occur?

....

....

*If the answer to the previous question was yes, d*id you and your partner ever talk about it

....

....

Did you feel like sex was a part of the relationship but not a part that you enjoyed?

....

....

....

....

How was this relationship different from others sexually?

....

....

....

....

❧ Back in Bed ❦

What does intimacy mean to me?

....
....
....

Were you in a sexually satisfying relationship?

....
....
....

I initiate sexual intimacy by

....
....
....
....

My ex initiated sexual intimacy by

....
....
....

I initiate emotional intimacy by..

....
....

My ex initiates emotional intimacy by

....
....
....

❧ Back in Bed ❧

I initiate physical intimacy by

....

....

....

....

I wanted my ex to…………………………………………………..……… but never asked.

Did you find yourself at times not present during sex?

....

....

....

....

....

If yes, Why?

....

....

....

....

....

Is this a sexual pattern?

....

....

....

....

Take a Minute to Review and Process

Sex can be loving, deeply passionate, intimate, and connected at times, but it can also be that you'd rather have a V8 at other times. You are the only person who really knows what is experienced fully in intimacy. As you revisit the memories of the bedroom, living room, kitchen, the floor, car, beach, closet, and other spaces of intimacy you shared with your ex, how does the memory of it make you feel? What are you thinking, wrestling with, regretting, grieving or just mad about? Did you deny, suppress, or betray your needs and or desires? Reflect on the lines below:

……………………………………………………………………………………………
……………………………………………………………………………………………
……………………………………………………………………………………………
……………………………………………………………………………………………
……………………………………………………………………………………………
……………………………………………………………………………………………
……………………………………………………………………………………………
……………………………………………………………………………………………
……………………………………………………………………………………………
……………………………………………………………………………………………
……………………………………………………………………………………………
……………………………………………………………………………………………
……………………………………………………………………………………………
……………………………………………………………………………………………
……………………………………………………………………………………………
……………………………………………………………………………………………

❧ *The End in sight* ☙

"So often the end of a love affair is death by a thousand cuts, so often its survival is life by a thousand stitches."
- Robert Brault

When it started to fall apart

Often when a relationship is starting to fall apart, there are signs. Some people will see them, ignore them, or just hope that the problems will go away. Pretending that a problem doesn't exist will not result in its disappearance. The next series of questions will re-examine the signs.

When did things start to fall apart? ……………………………………………………………..

Did you freeze, fight or take flight or check out? ……………………………………………….

When did the disagreements or conflict start to increase?………………………………………

When did the disagreements or conflict become constant?………………………………………

If the relationship was contentious from the beginning, did it escalate? ……………………..

Was there a point when you were always arguing and fighting? ………………………….…..
…………………………………………………………………………………………………
…………………………………………………………………………………………………
…………………………………………………………………………………………………

Was there a breakdown in communication and so you or your ex started to communicate less?………………………………………………………………………………………….…
…………………………………………………………………………………………………
…………………………………………………………………………………………………

The End in sight

When did one of you start to think that the other was needy?

....
....
....

When did you start lying to your ex?

....
....
....

When did your ex start lying to you?

....
....
....

What do you think was the cause of that?

....
....
....

When did it start to feel like a roommate instead of a significant other?

....
....
....

Was there a decrease in intimacy?

....
....
....

❦ *The End in sight* ❦

If so, did you discuss the decrease?..

....

....

....

....

Did you or your ex become suspicious or lose trust in each other?...........................

....

....

....

....

Did jealousy start to get the better of you or your ex?...

....

....

....

Was there a decrease in the time that you were spending together? When and why?

....

....

....

....

Did you or your ex give each other the silent treatment often?

....

....

....

The End in sight

Did you or your partner start to cut each other off when communicating and express irritation and annoyance when talking? ……………………………………………………………………
……………………………………………………………………………………………………
……………………………………………………………………………………………………
……………………………………………………………………………………………………

Did you notice sarcastic and critical tones when you communicated?
……………………………………………………………………………………………………
……………………………………………………………………………………………………
……………………………………………………………………………………………………
……………………………………………………………………………………………………

Did you start to just focus on the family or the kids and not each other?
……………………………………………………………………………………………………
……………………………………………………………………………………………………
……………………………………………………………………………………………………
……………………………………………………………………………………………………

When did your emotional needs stop being met? Were you feeling neglected and or abandoned? Was your ex feeling the same way? ……………………………………………
……………………………………………………………………………………………………
……………………………………………………………………………………………………
……………………………………………………………………………………………………
……………………………………………………………………………………………………

Were you being toxic in the relationship?……………………………………………………
……………………………………………………………………………………………………
……………………………………………………………………………………………………

The End in sight

When did you start feeling like the relationship was toxic?

....
....
....
....

When did you stop talking about the future?

....
....
....
....

When did you stop sharing your good news?

....
....
....
....

When did you start calling someone else when you needed empathy or comfort?

....
....
....

Did you feel like you started to disagree more than you agreed?

....
....
....
....

❦ *The End in sight* ❦

When did you start to feel drained by your ex?

....

....

....

Did your partner ever say that you were exhausted or draining?

....

....

....

Did you start to avoid spending time with your ex?

....

....

....

Did your ex start to avoid spending time with you?

....

....

....

Did you talk about it?

....

....

....

When did you stop laughing with each other?

....

....

....

✌ *The End in sight* ✌

When did you stop socializing?

....
....
....

Did you start to feel insecure?

....
....
....

When did either you or your ex start to open more time with family or friends instead of each other?

....
....

When did you start to feel alone even when you were together?

....
....
....

Did you start to feel like you settled or could do better?

....
....
....

Did you start feeling bored with the relationship?

....
....
....

The End in sight

Did you start to notice their flaws more than their strength?

....

....

When did you start convincing yourself you could make the relationship work?

....

....

....

When did you start to betray yourself to be in the relationship?

....

....

Did you find yourself thinking about leaving?

....

....

Why did you stay?

....

....

When did your needs change?

....

....

What were your changed needs?

....

....

....

Reflections

As you recall the signs and recognize things that you did not act on in your relationship, do you feel any regrets? If so, what are they?

Notes: ....
....
....
....
....
....
....

What makes you angry about your responses?

....
....
....
....

What do you have to forgive yourself or your ex for?

....
....
....
....

What are you not over yet or refuse to let go?

....
....
....
....
....

What do you have to accept?

....
....
....
....

What can you commit to change moving forward if the sign presents itself in the future?

....
....
....
....

What is very apparent to you now that you have looked back at those signs?

....
....
....
....

What did you miss?

....
....
....
....

What did you resist?

....
....
....
....

What did you ignore?

....
....
....
....

What did you recognize but just hoped would change?

....
....
....
....

What have you learned?

....
....
....
....
....
....
....
....
....
....
....
....
....

YESTERDAY

You once said
that we were
an unstoppable force,
and an immovable object.
Your thoughts,
now shaped perception,
stuck on stubborn.

You won't move. I don't budge.
I won't move. You don't budge.

Time
standing still,
our principles
stronger than
our wills.

I looked;
you saw.
You looked;
I paused.
In time,
no time.

I wish
the clock
could rewind,
to moments
when we
were free,

to love
and be,
the reason
we smiled.

Your harsh words burn.
My coldness turns,
your heart from mine
and mine from yours.

Oh how I miss,
when you could not
resist, my smile
that you now say is guile.

And yes, maybe
you see my lie,
the immovable force
of pride.

Your prejudice
denies what we once
called destiny
and forever's
now replaced
by never.

From the poetry book *"From My Heart and Rage to Yours"* By D'annie Grandison

❧ Goodbye ❧

A breakup is hard. Even when we see it coming, it still leaves us feeling a sense of loss. Sometimes we grieve the person, but sometimes we grieve a possibility that could have been. When we go through a breakup, the mere thought of reliving it makes us feel bad because we don't want to feel the pain we're trying to avoid. If we do not learn from mistakes or lessons, we are doomed to repeat the mistakes or be tested again to ensure we learned the lesson. In the pages below, write the story of B-day (Breakup Day)

The morning of my breakup I woke up feeling

....
....
....
....
....
....
....
....
....
....
....
....
....
....
....
....
....
....

That day ....

In the weeks that followed,

Since then

Circle the words that described your emotions that day.

ADD your own words to the chart as well

ABANDONED	AFRAID	ANGRY
ANXIETY	ASHAMED	BETRAYED
BITTER	BROKEN	BROKEN
DEPRESSED	DESPERATE	DISRESPECTED
FAKE	FRANTIC	GUILTY
HOPELESS	INSECURE	JEALOUS
LONELY	LOST	OBSESS
REJECTED	RESENTFUL	SHOCK
SICK	UNHAPPY	UPSET

Circle the words that describe how you feel today.

ADD your own words to the chart as well

ABANDONED	AFRAID	ANGRY
ANXIETY	ASHAMED	BETRAYED
BITTER	BROKEN	BROKEN
DEPRESSED	DESPERATE	DISRESPECTED
FAKE	FRANTIC	GUILTY
HOPELESS	INSECURE	JEALOUS
LONELY	LOST	OBSESS
REJECTED	RESENTFUL	SHOCK
SICK	UNHAPPY	UPSET

Reflection

How many of the emotions from the day you broke up did you circle on the chart for how you feel today? List the emotions you felt and still feel?

....
....
....
....
....

How did you deal with the emotions you felt?

....
....
....
....

How does this feel in comparison to previous relationships less or more intense?

....
....
....
....
....

What are some behaviors you used as a coping mechanism but realize now were not in your best interest?

....
....
....
....

Did you deal with or avoid the uncomfortable space?

....
....
....
....
....

Were you physically affected by the breakup? (weight gain or loss, physical pain, etc.)

....
....
....
....
....

Did you find yourself reacting or responding?

....
....
....

How did this relationship differ from the others?

....
....
....

What did it take from you?

....
....
....
....

What did it show you or teach you?

....
....
....
....
....
....

Did you take a break or try falling in love with someone easy to numb the pain?

....
....
....
....

Have you used the same processing, numbing, or rebounding after the previous relationship ended?

....
....

Did answering the questions make you question if your ex compared to your ex before? Is there a pattern?

....
....
....
....

What did I learn about how I handle

....
....?

How did I feel about myself when things were difficult? ....
....

How do I manage my hurt feelings? ....

What positives can I take from this experience? ....

What is something I would change if I could go back in time? ....
....

What are non-negotiable for me in terms of a partner? ....

What do I want from this separation that I don't have? ....
....

What do I Want? ....

What was my role in the breakup? ....

What do you think you brought to the relationship? ....

Is it possible that your expectations were too high? ....

Was I heartbroken? ....

What "pattern" do I see? ....

Where has this pattern shown up in other relationships and parts of my life? ....
....

What can I take responsibility for about what happened in my relationship?
....
....

Did I betray myself by denying my own needs? ....

Reflection

Before moving to the next section of the journal, spend a few minutes reflecting on how the emotional pain you've experienced affected you. Prepare for releasing the pain by saying aloud the statements given. This prepares your subconscious mind. For each question, think back to before you were hurt. Evaluate how much the following emotions have changed on a scale of 1 to 5.

- 1 - Not at all
- 2 - About 25% more
- 3 - About 50% more
- 4 - About 75% more
- 5 - 100% or more than before the hurt

1. **Anxiety**: ....

    Say aloud: Anxiety was chemically created by my body, and I will be able to reduce it.

2. **Depression**: ....

    Say aloud: Depression was chemically created by my body, and I will be able to reduce it.

3. **Hopelessness**: ....

    Say aloud: Hopelessness was chemically created by my body, and I will be able to reduce it.

4. **Mental Confusion**: ....

    Say aloud: Mental Confusion was chemically created by my body, and I will be able to reduce it.

❦ *Affirmations* ❦

- I give myself room to heal and grow from past wounds.

- I accept my feelings about previous injuries, but I will not allow myself to be imprisoned by them. I will move beyond the memories in my mind and my body.

- I understand it takes time to heal from betrayal, agony, and injustices.

- I accept that my past wounds are a part of who I am, but I also recognize that they are the result of past events, and I cannot allow them to continue to negatively impact my present and future.

- I clear my mind, spirit and body of negative emotions left over from past events.

- I forgive past injustices and those who hurt me for my sake. I meditate, pray, and even exercise to rid my body and mind of any stress.

- My spirit will remain strong despite the past.

- I am integrated with the ebb and flow of the universe. I accept that life brings both positive and negative experiences. This acceptance enables me to grow. Things happen for me, not to me.

- Whether I am enjoying good times or life is less than ecstatic, I will try to find the benefit from each experience.

- ***Today, I am safe and whole.*** I have inner balance. I recognize my ability to overcome the past and look forward to a bright future.

❧ *Moving on* ❧

The journey of a thousand miles begins with the first step.

Affirmation

- I can be in full control of my emotions and thoughts.

- I can direct or redirect my thoughts.

- I will try to choose thoughts that serve me. I can choose to have a thought that serves me or impedes me.

- In difficult times, I am focused on solutions, self-care, and grace.

- I'm doing my best, and if I'm not, I'll try even harder.

- In pleasant times, I will enjoy focus and be grateful for the experience

- Negative emotions are signs that something needs to be corrected, purged, or challenged.

- Although it can be challenging to control my thoughts and emotions at times, I will challenge myself to push beyond my comfort zone.

THE AFTERMATH AFTER THE BREAKUP

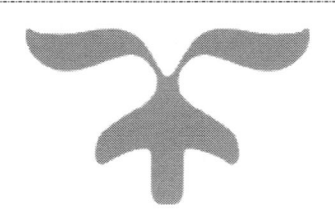

I wake up in the mornin' and I wonder
Why everything the same as it was
I can't understand, no
I can't understand

How life goes on the way it does
Why does my heart go on beating
Why do these eyes of mine cry
Don't they know it's the end of the world
It ended when you said goodbye

Skeeter Davis

❧ *After my break-up* ❧

After my break-up I woke up each day feeling like

....
....
....
....

What I missed most was

....
....
....
....

What I missed the least was

....
....
....
....

These feelings brought back old feelings of

....
....
....
....

I allowed or did not allow myself to cry because

....
....
....

❧ *After my break-up* ❦

I felt like I wanted revenge because

....
....
....
....

I wanted to take revenge by

....
....
....
....

I did or did not take revenge because

....
....
....
....

I was kind or unkind to myself after the break up because

....
....
....
....
....
....
....

❧ *After my break-up* ☙

What I'm holding on to, get distracted by, and that I'm really struggling to let go of is

……………………………………………………………………………………………
……………………………………………………………………………………………
……………………………………………………………………………………………
……………………………………………………………………………………………

I spent time going on my ex's social media, calling, texting, driving by my ex's house, apartment, job, family property because

……………………………………………………………………………………………
……………………………………………………………………………………………
……………………………………………………………………………………………
……………………………………………………………………………………………

I spent a lot of time alone or avoiding being alone because

……………………………………………………………………………………………
……………………………………………………………………………………………
……………………………………………………………………………………………
……………………………………………………………………………………………
……………………………………………………………………………………………

I struggled with denial or letting go because

……………………………………………………………………………………………
……………………………………………………………………………………………
……………………………………………………………………………………………
……………………………………………………………………………………………
……………………………………………………………………………………………

❧ *After my break-up* ❧

I dealt with the pain/I avoided the pain by

....
....
....
....
....

This break up made me feel like I was not enough, which is the way I felt when

....
....
....
....
....

This break up made me feel abandoned, which is the way I felt when

....
....
....
....
....

This break up made me feel like I was rejected, which is the way I felt when

....
....
....
....
....

❧ *After my break-up* ☙

I distracted myself by

....
....
....
....
....

I had hookups or rebounds in an attempt to not feel the pain

....
....
....
....
....

I spent a lot of time alone or avoiding being alone

....
....
....
....
....

What I needed to have closure was

....
....
....
....
....

❧ *After my break-up* ☙

What was I denied of?

．．

．．

．．

．．

．．

What did I need in the relationship that you did not get?

．．

．．

．．

．．

．．

What is an area of identity I struggle with as a result of the breakup?

．．

．．

．．

．．

．．

What did you learn from your break-up about how you handle conflicts, confrontations, or indifferences?

．．

．．

．．

．．

After my break-up

Do I struggle to receive or give love?

....
....
....
....
....

How did the breakup affect my self-esteem?

....
....
....
....
....

What is the pattern that I recognize in this and my previous relationships?

....
....
....
....
....

I judge myself or blame myself for

....
....
....
....
....

❧ *After my break-up* ☙

I judge or blame my ex for

....
....
....

I take full responsibility for

....
....
....

I wish my ex would take responsibility for

....
....
....

I cannot forgive my ex for

....
....
....
....
....
....

What has my last relationship made me realize that I want from my next relationship?

....
....
....
....

❧ *THE LAST TALK THAT NEVER HAPPENED* ❧

Imagine that you are having a conversation with your ex. Ask the following questions, then imagine the response. Repeat the exercise by asking yourself the questions that apply.

Can you give me the full truth?

....
....
....

When were we done in your mind?

....
....
....

How did you know this wasn't going to work?

....
....
....

What do you think went wrong?

....
....
....

Were you ever unfaithful?

....
....
....

THE LAST TALK THAT NEVER HAPPENED

Do you think I was unfaithful?

....

....

....

Do you think we both contributed to this ending?

....

....

....

What do you think my best qualities are?

....

....

....

Do you think I deserved you?

....

....

....

Did you think you deserved me?

....

....

Do you think we are different people than we were when we first met?

....

....

....

THE LAST TALK THAT NEVER HAPPENED

How would you describe our breakup to friends?

....

....

....

Do you think we should distance ourselves for a while?

....

....

....

Do you wish we never met?

....

....

....

What do you think you brought to our relationship?

....

....

....

....

....

....

....

....

....

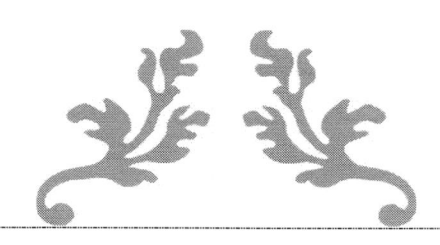

CRY IF YOU NEED TO, CRY IF YOU NEED TO

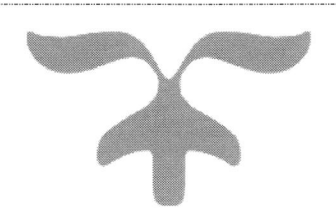

Harsh Reality Self-Reflection Questions:

In what situations am I most challenged when it comes to letting go of my hurt?

....
....
....

Am I aware of when it is time to release myself from my emotional pain?

....
....
....

Am I a forgiving person?

....
....

Am I passive aggressive?

....
....

Am I where I want to be to get the person I deserve?

....
....
....

Is there a story I tell myself and do I use it as a reason to lower the bar when I date?

....
....
....

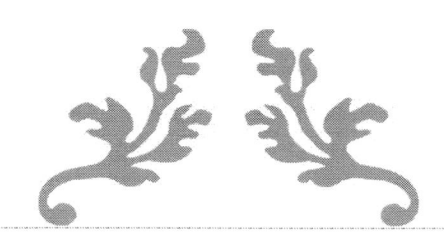

FORGIVE THEM, FORGIVE YOURSELF, OVER AND OVER AGAIN UNTIL THERE IS NOTHING LEFT TO FORGIVE

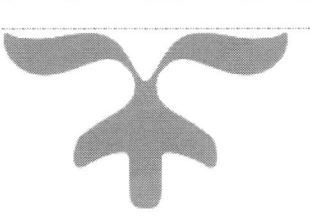

❧ *I WILL LEARN TO FORGIVE NOT FOR MY EX'S SAKE BUT FOR MY FREEDOM* ❦

I will try until I learn to forgive my ex. I let go of negativity from previous experiences and set myself free from the prison of grudges, pain, and anger towards my ex and all the others who trigger those emotions in my body.

....
....

I remove the bitterness from my heart and mind. Holding onto this pain is unnecessary, unproductive, and keeps me a victim of my past. I want to move forward into a life without it.

....
....

I eliminate the desire for revenge from my heart as I allow God, the universe, and karma to handle things instead. I am tired of fighting this battle.

....
....

I know that it is important to let go and make peace. I reject past pain and anger. I do not want to ruminate in blame and residual sadness.

....
....

I notice the lightness I feel after letting go of the past, anger, and resentment, which allows me to find joy again because I forgive.

....
....

❧ *I WILL LEARN TO FORGIVE NOT FOR MY EX'S SAKE BUT FOR MY FREEDOM* ❧

I forgive myself, too. I am doing the best I can and will continue to do better.

....
....

I will rid myself of the constant reminders of previous mistakes and errors that I made. I will do what I can to make up for my mistakes, learn from them, and move on with a lighter heart.

....
....

I acknowledge my feelings and strive daily to forgive until there is nothing to forgive.

Today, I will show myself forgiveness and move on from my past. I will stop allowing the past to control me and my present.

....
....
....

Emotions, thoughts, beliefs, and the chemical nature of your body make it difficult to let go of the past, be free of it, and forgive. Because memories stay with you, the key to healing is releasing the anger and resentment associated with the event.

....
....
....

The deepest wounds require us to sit and allow the pain to pass through us at times, but this is difficult to do when we hold on to the pain. Many people are resistant to forgiveness because they don't understand what forgiveness is or isn't.

....
....
....

"What Forgiveness Is Not" Pledges

Forgiveness is not about the other person. When I forgive someone, including myself I'm not saying that person has no responsibility for what happened. Their actions caused pain, and yes, they are responsible for that pain.

- Even if they completely accept the responsibility for their actions, that doesn't take away My pain. Even if they tell me how sorry they are 100 times, that won't take away my pain.

- I am the one who holds that pain, and I am the one who will need to let it go. No, it's not fair, but it is true.

Forgiveness is completely about me. It's about my freedom, my peace, and my wellbeing.

❧ *Forgiveness is not about staying with someone who is toxic.* ☙

A major misconception about forgiveness is that you must be with the person who harmed you, even if that person is toxic.

- You don't need to be with someone who emotionally, physically, or sexually abuses you, lies continually, is drunk or high much of the time, or steals from you, whether they steal things, your self-respect, or your dignity.

- You don't have to be friends with or spend time with people who cause you to feel terrible about yourself. Forgiveness doesn't require this.

My job is to care for myself and those I'm responsible for. I can forgive the person, release the anger and emotional pain, and never see them again.

....
....
....
....
....
....
....
....
....
....
....

Forgiveness isn't giving away your power or making you weak. *Making a choice to forgive someone is one of the most powerful things you can do for yourself.*

Harsh Reality Reflection

What is your biggest concern about forgiving your ex?
....
....
....

Everyone has done something they are ashamed of. What is your biggest fear if you forgive yourself?
....
....

How can I forgive my ex and other exes for which I still harbor unforgiving feelings?
....
....
....

Where can I get more help to learn forgiveness?
....
....
....

What can I do to make it easier for me to forgive and move on?
....
....
....

What are some offenses that I find difficult to forgive my ex for?
....
....
....

❧ Harsh Reality Reflection ☙

When I am no longer saddled with the pain of "it," I'll be able to:

....
....
....

Write out why a future without emotional pain is better than feeling the way you do now.

....
....
....

How has my preoccupation with the past harmed me and my life?

....
....
....

What would I do right now without the burden of the past?

....
....
....

How do I allow the past to affect my future?

....
....
....

After forgiveness, have you ever experienced grief?

....
....

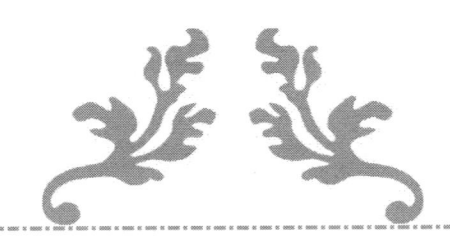

Stages of Grief: Denial, Anger, Bargaining, Depression, Acceptance... Next

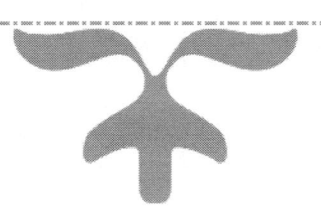

The stages of grief can be different for everyone, but at some point, we all walk through portals of anger, denial, bargaining, depression, why me, yearning for it to end, acceptance and, finally, a lesson. In the questions below, explain what you went through for each stage and list the ways in which you tried to get through it, got through it or is still struggling with it today.

Denial..
....
....
....
....

Anger..
....
....
....
....
....
....
....
....

Bargaining..
....
....
....
....
....

Depression..
....
....
....
....
....
....

Yearning for the pain to end
....
....
....
....

Why Me?
....
....
....
....
....
....
....

Acceptance..
....
....
....
....

Lesson

What will I do differently next time?

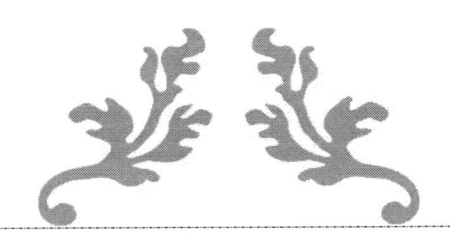

THIS TIME
WAS SUPPOSED
TO BE DIFFERENT
BUT
WAS IT REALLY
JUST THE SAME?

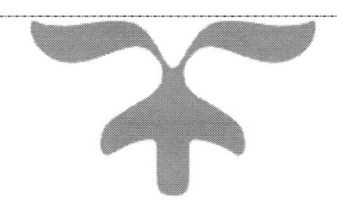

Haunted

I don't fear failure

what I fear are regrets.

The ones that keep

me up at nights.

The ones I can't shake

because I knew better.

The regrets that haunt me

when I reflect

on the exact moment,

I could have made

another choice,

but instead

chose you.

My poison,

my mistake,

my unhappily ever after.

It's hard to live with

a knowing,

a hoping,

a wanting

for you to be anything

but the mistake

you live

in my memory as.

You are the proof

that mistakes

are real,

and so are thieves.

You stole happiness

and piece of my heart

that never belonged to you.

You left shattered pieces behind

and evidence of betrayal

while you escaped.

❧ MY POISON ☙

What once was,

is no more.

Congratulations,

you

evened the score.

Pierced

me to my core.

I thought I was someone

you adore.

I saw in you
what I hoped you'd be
while you asked,

why me?

Unaware your fears

left a tear

in MY

at-must-fear.

You ran away from

what haunts you,

it now haunts me.

The inability

to allow trust,

not to be crushed

by the dust

of deceit

leaving droplets of shit;

I mean regrets

of me knowing that

I can't blame you

just me

because I chose you,

my poison

From the poetry book From "My Heart And Rage to Yours" 2nd Edition

by D'annie Grandison

Would I know if my relationship was toxic? Toxicity assessment

Control	sometimes	often	always
How often did your ex show controlling behavior?	☐	☐	☐
Did your ex always want to have things their way?	☐	☐	☐
Did you always want to have things your way?	☐	☐	☐
Did your ex insist on going with you when you spent time with your friends?	☐	☐	☐
Did you insist on going with your ex when they spent time with your friends?	☐	☐	☐
Did your ex need to be the center of attention?	☐	☐	☐
Did you always need to be the center of attention?	☐	☐	☐
Did your ex-refuse to accept blame even when it's obviously their fault?	☐	☐	☐
Did you refuse to accept blame even when it's obviously your fault?	☐	☐	☐
Did your ex limit whom you're allowed to see or when?	☐	☐	☐
Did you limit whom your ex was allowed to see or when?	☐	☐	☐

Distrust. sometimes often always

Did your ex doubt everything you say? ☐ ☐ ☐

Was your word never good enough? ☐ ☐ ☐

Did you doubt everything your ex said? ☐ ☐ ☐

Was their word never good enough? ☐ ☐ ☐

Did your ex track your location with a phone app? ☐ ☐ ☐

Did you track your ex your location with a phone app? ☐ ☐ ☐

Did your ex quiz you to try to catch you in a lie? ☐ ☐ ☐

Did you quiz your ex to try to catch them in a lie? ☐ ☐ ☐

Do you have to justify yourself all the time? ☐ ☐ ☐

Did you make your ex justify themselves all of the time? ☐ ☐ ☐

Justifying your partner's behavior. sometimes often always

Did you have to explain your partner's behavior to others? ☐ ☐ ☐

Did your ex justify your behavior to others? ☐ ☐ ☐

Was your ex rude and disrespectful? ☐ ☐ ☐

Are you rude and disrespectful? ☐ ☐ ☐

Physical or verbal abuse. sometimes   often   always

Was your ex abusive in any way?   ☐   ☐   ☐

Did you abuse your ex in any way?   ☐   ☐   ☐

Passive-aggressive behavior. sometimes   often   always

Was your ex passive-aggressive?   ☐   ☐   ☐

Were you passive-aggressive?   ☐   ☐   ☐

Did your ex neglect or forget things that were important to you?   ☐   ☐   ☐

Did you neglect or forget things that were important to you?   ☐   ☐   ☐

Did you receive a lot of excuses from your partner in general?   ☐   ☐   ☐

Did you give your partner a lot of excuses in general?   ☐   ☐   ☐

Lying.   sometimes   often   always

Did your ex lie to you often?   ☐   ☐   ☐

Did you lie to your ex often?   ☐   ☐   ☐

Did your partner lie to you to keep the peace?   ☐   ☐   ☐

Did you lie to your partner to keep the peace?   ☐   ☐   ☐

Did your ex lie in order to avoid spending time with you?   ☐   ☐   ☐

Did you lie in order to avoid spending time with your ex?   ☐   ☐   ☐

Notes:

Past behaviors can be a good predictor of current and future behavior. At times it is hard for us to see our patterns, recognize our blind spots and break free from the cycle we are a part of and fail to see. In the table below, select "Yes" if you agree, and "No" if you disagree or unsure if you are not sure of it could be maybe

Questions	Yes	No	Unsure
Do you attract the same type of person?			
You picked someone not on the same life path career-wise			
You picked someone not on the same path financial wise			
You picked someone not on the same level educationally			
You picked someone you could be the teacher for and are smarter than			
You picked someone whom you made exceptions for right away			
You gave up parts of your identity to align with your ex			
You pushed or violated your emotional boundary to accommodate			
You were not satisfied sexually but bypassed that for your ex's satisfaction			
You picked someone who shut down often or used passive aggressive behavior			
You picked someone who pressed your buttons			
You picked someone whose buttons you could press			
You ignored your increased anxiety when you around your ex			
You picked someone who was disrespectful			
You picked someone you were allowed to disrespect			
You stopped spending time with your family and friends			
You were hurt because you spent too much time with their family or friends			

Questions	Yes	No	Unsure
You started out fast and quick			
You said I love you first			
You withheld your feelings			
You picked someone who withheld their feelings			
You cheated			
You were cheated on			
You didn't trust your ex			
You picked someone with trust issues			
You carried your fear of abandonment in the relationship			
You picked someone with abandonment issues			
You found yourself in a relationship that became purely physical			
You picked someone who had a hard time being vulnerable with you			
You had a hard time being vulnerable with your ex			
You blamed your ex for a lot of the issues in the relationship			
Your ex blames you for a lot of the issues in the relationship			
You felt insecure in your relationship			
You picked someone who felt insecure in the relationship			
You picked someone that required constant validation			
You picked someone that required constant nurturing			
You picked someone that never validated you			
You picked someone that was not very nurturing			
You were very protective of your ex			
You picked someone that you never felt protected by			

Questions	Yes	No	Unsure
You were very criticizing of your ex			
You picked someone that was very critical of you			
You did not talk about your past with your ex			
You over shared with your ex			
Your ex didn't talk about the past			
Your ex spoke too much about the past			
You picked someone with commitment issues			
You had commitment issues with your ex			
You picked someone who didn't meet your own expectations			
You picked someone whom you didn't meet their criteria			
You picked someone who was abusive			
You picked someone who had an addictive personality			
You picked someone who had an addiction			
You picked someone whom you had to constantly reassure			
You picked someone who wasn't reassuring			
You picked someone you thought you could make you love you			
You picked someone who had an unresolved issue with mother/father			
You recognized traits of your mother/father in your ex			
You picked someone who still harbors anger towards an ex			
You picked someone who was ok with you harboring anger towards your ex			
You picked someone that was clingy			
You picked someone who allowed you to be clingy			
You picked someone super independent			

Questions	Yes	No	Unsure
You picked someone dependent			
You picked someone with a strong personality			
You picked a bully			
You picked someone who allowed you to be a bully			
You picked someone smile			
You picked someone cocky			
You picked someone who was way different from you			
You picked someone who is just like you			
You picked a fixer-upper, someone you could fix or change			
You picked an alpha			
You picked someone who was codependent			
You picked someone who could really see through you			
You picked someone you could easily hide in front of			
You picked someone you admired and wanted to be like			
You picked someone who you were more "together" than			
You picked someone because of their looks			
You allowed someone to pick you because of your looks			
You broke a non-negotiable for the person you picked			
You picked a dominant person because you are submissive			
You picked a submissive person because you are dominant			
You picked a controlling person			
You were petty			

Questions	Yes	No	Unsure
You picked someone who snaps easily			
You picked someone who allowed you to snap without leaving you			
You picked a person who allowed youth to be controlling			
You picked a chatter box			
You picked someone who accepts you being a chatterbox			
You picked someone who came on very strong			
You picked someone that was the jealous type			
You picked someone who was a double standard			
You picked someone who allowed you to be a double standard			
You picked someone secretive			
You picked someone unpredictable			
You picked someone you could lie to or hide secrets			
You picked a narcissist			
You picked an empath			
You picked an empath because you are a narcissist			
Total			

On this page, after the questions, create a tally sheet with categories of responses and with a number of answers per section.

Reflection:

IT WASN'T JUST YOU. IT WAS ALSO ME. SO NOW WHAT?

CHAOS
By D'annie Grandison from "My heart and Rage to Yo"

You left; I stayed.
You stayed; I left.
You packed.
I unpacked.

You took back
moments,
I took back
dreams.

We
deferred,
obliterated
rejected and
abandoned
everything
we were for
and to each other

We were like raisins
in the sun,
beaten
by drops
of pain,
no gain.
What was,

now slain,
could be?
won't be.
Not you,
not me.
No us?
just 'cuss,
on cusp
of hate,
dislike,
disdain.

No we,
just you
or me.

No we?
No
Bliss?
No
miss
no chance,
no time.

No rhyme
or reason,
your love
now treason.

What was
can't be,
should be
won't be,
just free
to be
No this.
No that.
No-thing
No
Ring
No
tomorrow.

In the last section, we looked at some of the patterns and cycles that could be in the ways how you selected your ex. Recognizing and taking accountability for our actions adds to the growth process. If we are to grow into more self-aware individuals, we must be able to recognize limitations in others as well as limitations and areas for improvement in ourselves.

In this section, you will look at your role in the relationship space you occupied. We will also look at your expectations or standards for your relationship. By focusing on areas that are critical to the success of a relationship.

❧ *Communication* ☙

It has been said that communication is the key to a successful relationship; however, keys do not work for locks that they are not right for. Communication is a two-way street. There is good communication and bad communication. A good communicator listens. If you and your ex differed in communication and listening styles, the relationship would have experienced strains as a result.

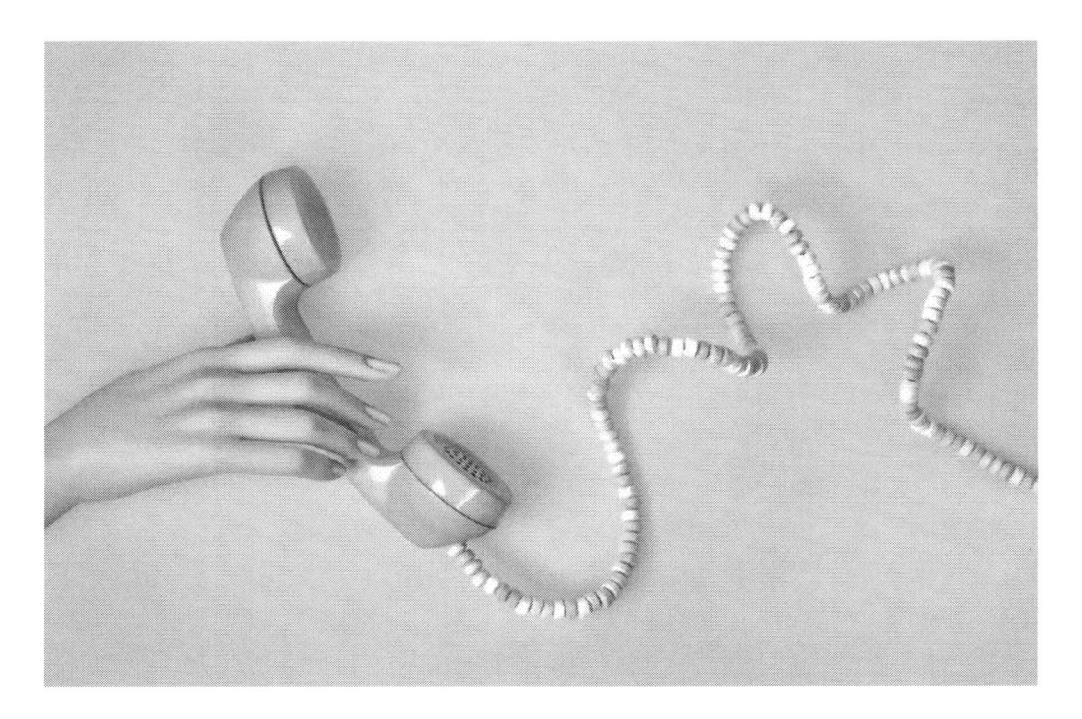

"To give out someone else's secret is a betrayal. To give out yours is stupidity."
Voltaire

Write on the line if you or your ex used this communication method. If you or your ex did not use the communication skill listed, then write the reasons.

1. **Be open and honest with one another.** When I was open and honest, it was free of rage and anger. I was able to be open while not causing my partner distress. I was mindful and used kind words and the tone of my words.

   ....
   ....
   ....
   ....
   ....

2. **Be open and honest with one another.** When My EX was open and honest, it was free of rage and anger. He was able to be open while not causing my partner distress. My EX was mindful of their words.

   ....
   ....
   ....
   ....
   ....

3. I often used **Passive-aggressive behavior,** which is a pattern of indirectly expressing negative feelings. I was sometimes resentful, procrastinated intentionally to irritate or hurt my ex, responded in a condescending or cynical tone and frequently complained that I was not being appreciated.

   ....
   ....
   ....
   ....
   ....

4. My ex often used **Passive-aggressive behavior,** which is a pattern of indirectly expressing negative feelings. My ex was sometimes resentful, procrastinated intentionally to irritate or hurt my ex, responded in a condescending or cynical tone and frequently complained that they were not being appreciated.

....
....
....
....

5. **You are saying, but that's not what you mean.** Did you ever use mind-reading with your ex because you did not trust that what they said was what they meant? Did you have to decode or translate because you did trust their words? Did you feel like, based on gestures, tones or cues, the words did not match up with your feeling or interpretation? As a result, did you have to deduce and conclude what your ex really meant?

....
....
....
....

6. **You are saying, but that's not what you mean.** Did your ex ever use mind-reading with you because they did not trust that what you said was what you meant? Did your ex have to decode or translate because they did not trust your words? Did they feel like, based on gestures, tones or cues, the words did not match up with your feeling or interpretation? As a result, did they have to deduce and conclude what you really meant?

....
....
....
....

7. **Listened to respond or react not to hear.** Did you find yourself rehearsing your response or pacing your reaction when you were talking to your ex? Did you filter out the information? Did you miss out on some key details of what your ex was trying to say as a result?

   ....
   ....
   ....
   ....
   ....
   ....

8. Do you think that there were times when your ex was rehearsing responses or pacing their reaction when you were talking to them? Did they miss out on some key details of what you were trying to say as a result?

   ....
   ....
   ....
   ....
   ....
   ....

9. Did you find yourself often blaming and judging while you listened? How did you handle feelings of negativity, shame or embarrassment you experienced while communicating with your ex? Did you stop listening and execute a behavior or action in retaliation?

   ....
   ....
   ....
   ....
   ....
   ....

10. Did you find that your ex often used blaming and judging while they listened? How do you think they handle feelings of negativity, shame, or embarrassment they experienced while communicating with you? Did they stop listening and execute a behavior or action in retaliation?

....
....
....
....
....
....
....
....
....

❧ The Teacher Lecturer ☙

When your ex spoke, did you often interrupt because what they were saying was wrong, very wrong? Did you often jump in with the right way or advice? "You need to," "Why don't you?"

....
....
....
....
....
....
....
....
....
....

Communication Chart

Communication	Never	Sometimes	Always
I used judgment words			
I used generalizations during arguments			
I used blaming or accusatory words			
I brought up old issues			
I used comparison			
I hit below the belt			
I used either or thinking			
I brushed things under the rug			
I ignored my partner when I was upset			
I made assumptions easily			
I raised my voice when we argue			
I often thought before I spoke			
I was flexible and compromised			
I felt like my ex didn't understand my position			
I was irritated			
I yelled a lot			
I often stated by hurt feelings			
I dismissed my partner verbally			
I responded with belittling words			
I used guilt-tripping when I didn't get my way			
I used my words as a weapon			
I used "should" when we argued			

❧ Communication Chart ❧

Review your answers from the previous charts. What can you admit about yourself based on your honest responses?

....
....
....
....
....

What do you need to work on or improve?

....
....
....
....
....

What ways did you communicate that did not serve you or the relationship?

....
....
....
....
....

What ways did you and your ex communicate that did not serve you or the relationship?

....
....
....
....

❧ Communication Chart ❧

Examine the areas that did not serve you and or the relationship. In what other relationships have you used these communication skills. Complete the chart below by checking off the communication and the selection of the person you have used that same method of communication with.

Communication	Family	Exes	Friends
I use judgmental words			
I use generalizations during arguments			
I use blaming or accusatory words			
I bring up old issues			
I used comparison			
I hit below the belt			
I use either or thinking			
I brush things under the rug			
I ignore when I am upset			
I make assumptions easily			
I raise my voice when we argue			
I am flexible and compromised			
I feel like my position isn't understood			
I am often irritated			
I yell a lot			
I often stated by hurt feelings			
I dismiss verbally			
I responded with belittling words			
I used guilt-tripping when I didn't get my way			
I used my words as a weapon			
I used should when we argued			

❧ *Communication Chart* ❧

What are the similarities and differences you notice with the charts and between the charts?

....

....

....

....

What are the ways in which you communicate with people in general?

....

....

....

....

....

What do you want to change about it?

....

....

....

....

....

What do you want to keep the same?

....

....

....

....

....

What any anger issue do you recognize, and what do you think the source of that anger is?

....

....

When You Can No Longer Run From The Past, Turn Around And Face It.

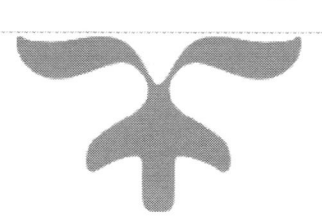

The Haunting Past

Physical, emotional, sexual, psychological, and sociological issues from childhood play a significant role in adulthood. Emotional abuse, neglect, abandonment, family substance abuse issues, mental illness, parental separation or divorce, or family tragedy such as death, leaves an imprint in your body that operates in the background with or without your knowledge.

When these emotions and energies are in our bodies, it can cause a certain familiarity and bond with situations and people that are unhealthy. It can even lead to feelings of serendipity. This is due to the trauma identity latching on to a person whose personality feeds the negative emotion that the trauma stitched into our bodies.

When we choose to be with people who see the issues but try to avoid them by convincing you that we can change them or that this time will be different, it only leads to the perpetuation of cycles of dysfunction, hurt, and disappointment.

Exploring your childhood issues and the role it plays in your adulthood is an important way to assess the types of relationships you get into, as well as the parts of you that you will feed or starve. If you were neglected as a child, it is possible that you could choose relationships that will allow you to hide, not be seen, avoid closeness and support the feelings of neglect you still carry from childhood.

The way we form our identity is largely dependent on our childhood experiences. Knowing that we are good enough can be a lifelong challenge if that foundation was not engrained during childhood. Our interpretation of the world and ourselves comes from whom we were told we were verbally, through actions or inactions.

Early trauma, neglect and abuse affect the brain, mind, body, and spirit. When we are not healing or healed, navigating a healthy relationship can be a struggle. When we were never given emotional safety, it is not the instinct to look for it. There is a part of us that knows we can survive without it, so we let the situation play out and hope for the best, despite evidence that it may not.

"Who controls the past controls the future. Who controls the present controls the past."
(George Orwell)

"There is no past we can bring back by longing for it. There is only an eternal now that builds and creates out of the past something new and better."
(Johann Wolfgang von Goethe)

In the chart below, list the areas that you experienced in childhood. Check the boxes of the other places those issues show up in your relationships and other places

Childhood Issue	Experience with exes	Experience with others	Experience During my childhood
Sexual abuse			
Physical abuse			
Mental Abuse			
Neglect			
Domestic Violence			
Substance abuse			
Illness			
Death of a loved one			
Divorced			
Abandonment			
Medical Condition			
Poverty			
Violence			
War			
Stress			
Rape			
Incarceration			
Intense Fear			
Hyper-vigilance			
Accident			

Answer the questions regarding how you have been affected by the following childhood trauma aftermath

Do you struggle with hyper-vigilance?

....
....
....
....

Do you struggle with trusting your partner?

....
....
....
....

Do you struggle with a loss of control?

....
....
....
....

Do you have physical health problems because of these issues?

....
....
....

Do you struggle with fatigue, anxiety or depression?

....
....
....

Do you struggle with overthinking?

....
....
....
....

What are some of the ways your childhood trauma shows up in your relationships?

....
....
....
....

What are some of the challenges you deal with as a result?

....
....
....
....

What steps have you taken towards your healing?

....
....
....
....

If you have not taken any steps or sought help, what prevents you from doing so?

....
....
....
....

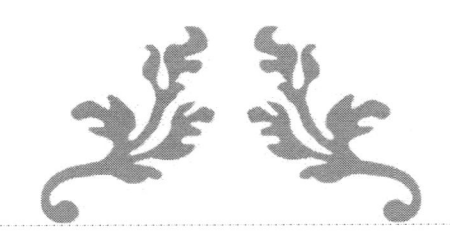

AM I READY FOR LOVE, OR DO I JUST WANT TO BE APPEASED?

To recognize things, you may suppress, bypass, and/or may be unaware of, let us examine some reoccurring themes that could show up in your relationship as a result of you not dealing with your past.

Do you find yourself not communicating your feelings to your partner? Give an example.

....
....
....
....

How does this non-communication serve or hurt you?

....
....
....
....
....

How angry do you get inside when this happens?

....
....
....
....
....

How does this anger show up?

....
....
....
....
....

How do you hide it? (The anger)

....
....
....
....

How do you normally avoid or deny it?

....
....
....
....

Are you denying it now?

....
....
....
....

How does this anger make you feel about yourself, others, and life in general?

....
....
....
....

The next time this happens, watch yourself from an observer witness point of view. Do not judge. Just watch. What did you observe?

....
....
....
....

What triggered the emotions?

....
....
....
....

Do you feel like you are experiencing feelings from childhood or previous relationship when you are triggered?

....
....
....
....

How can you tell if your fight or flight response has been activated?

....
....
....
....

What does that look like from the outside (fight or flight)?

....
....
....
....
....
....
....
....

Describe your behavior or actions when you:

Fight:

....
....
....
....
....

Flight:

....
....
....
....
....

Freeze:

....
....
....
....
....

Feel Ashamed:

....
....
....
....
....

Feel ignored, rejected, belittled by your partner directly or indirectly:

....
....
....
....
....

What does that feel like from the inside?

....
....
....
....

Did you try to get out of the emotion or through it?

....
....
....
....

Do you try to soothe yourself when you are triggered? What are some ways that you can self soothe when you are amid the feeling of perceived abandonment, neglect, rejection or non-valued?

How do you know if something is happening to you or for you?

....
....
....
....
....

How do you feel when you do not have things in a certain way?

....

....

How do you respond when you do not have things in a certain way?

....

....

When you do not get your way, do you feel like the person ALWAYS do this as opposed to them doing this right now, at this moment?

....

....

....

....

When you don't get what you want, how much of that feeling comes from the moment you are being denied what you want versus what is coming from a place that is familiar (childhood, past relationship with family friends or romantic relationships)?

....

....

....

....

What have you done to work on some of the things you do in a relationship that does not serve the relationship in a healthy way?

....

....

....

Was it me, you, or us? Do I know what I want? Do I know what I need?

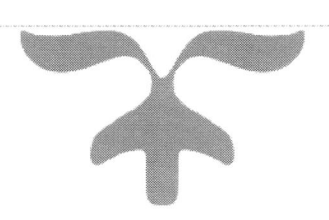

Struggle Puzzle

By D'ANNIE GRANDISON FROM MY HEART AND RAGE TO YOURS 2ND EDITION

Real love measured

by this struggle,

I guess we got

ourselves a puzzle.

You've gone from having

joy in the face

To permanence of

hating this place.

But I'm stuck,

dwelling in this cold space,

Now love and irritation

are tied in a race.

No more time to keep

up with this pace.

I know you see old

rage in my face.

I guess this is how it feels

when you fall from grace.

One day, maybe we will have to

hear each other's case,

But I can't now

that I'm in this manic.

I can't be distracted

by the panic,

questions, innuendos, and dramatics,

Premeditated assumptions and schematics.

.

We all want the perfect partner who will accept us for who we are, but what if the acceptance of who we are is *where* we are and not *who*? Are you where you want to be in your personal growth and development trajectory?

....
....
....
....
....

Where you are right now, is that what you want your partner to accept? Are you willing to accept your partner where they are even if they are not where you want them to be? What are some characteristics you pick next?

....
....
....
....
....

R3. Read, Reflect, remind yourself of the traits you possess or lack, the traits you select or accept in a partner and the traits you desire deeply and will look for in your next relationship.

....
....
....
....
....

Complete the chart on the following page.

❧ This is Me ❦

STATMENT	AGREE	DISAGREE	DEBATABLE
I am open and can take constructive criticism.			
I can be described as a kind and warm person.			
I always try to find a positive side of a situation			
I do not beat around the bush, and I am very direct			
I am not lazy, and I spend energy working, not pretending to.			
When and if I am given a task, I can see it through and use appropriate checks and balance systems, due diligence and thoroughness			
I can be described as unselfish			
I am fun and engage in activities outside my comfort zone			
I am not just tunnel visioned with my own values and way of thinking. I can put myself in someone else's shoes even if it completely differs from view.			
I am self-disciplined, driven and ambitious			
I am not lazy			
I do not procrastinate			
I prefer to be in control of a situation			

CONTENT	AGREE	DISAGREE	DEBATABLE
I am where I want to be financially in life			
I am where I want to be emotionally in life			
I have done enough work on my issues			
I want someone			
I need to love someone			
If I were to date, I would be exactly who I want to be			
I consider my life to be in order			
I am shallow			
I am vain			
I need financial security to feel love			
It is easy for me to trust			
I think compromise is the same as submitting			
I think my way of thinking is better at solving problems than most people			
I could be described as condescending			
I am humble, modest, and shy			
I require acknowledgment and validation			
I say I do not need acknowledgment or validation, but it bothers me when I do not get it from my partner			
I am sexually open to trying new things with my partner			

CONTENT	AGREE	DISAGREE	DEBATABLE
When I am in love, I am on a high			
When a relationship doesn't work out, I am devastated to my core			
I want my relationship to end with happily ever after			
I get bored easily if my partner doesn't stimulate me constantly			
I am reserved, low energy and not overly animated			
I am passionate, intense and externalize emotionally, often			
I am Self-conscious, so I look deep into what people may really think, feel, or say about me			
I am impulsive and unpredictable			
I have anxiety that requires me to explain to my partner that they need to be mindful of my triggers, mood swings, and irrational responses at times.			
I do not like to be vulnerable.			
When I'm shown vulnerability, it makes me know that they really care			
I need my space to be alone without having to explain to my partner what I am going through.			
I get angry, say things I don't really like and feel bad about it often.			

CONTENT	AGREE	DISAGREE	DEBATABLE
I am sometimes emotionally unstable			
I am secure, confident, and completely authentic			
I often experience jealousy			
I would want my son or daughter to date, marry and have children with a person like			
I am honest with others			
I am honest with myself			

Review the questions and answers you just selected. Answer the series of questions below about your choices.

What emotions did you feel as you were answering the questions?

....
....
....

How honest were you with your answers?

....
....
....

Did you struggle with your responses?

....
....
....

❧ This is Me ❧

What did the answers reveal?

....
....
....

Explain in detail what you realized about yourself, what you have to offer, what you could improve on and what you plan to do about your realizations.

....
....
....
....
....
....
....
....
....
....
....
....
....
....

What role do you think the answers played in your past and previous relationships?

....
....
....
....
....
....

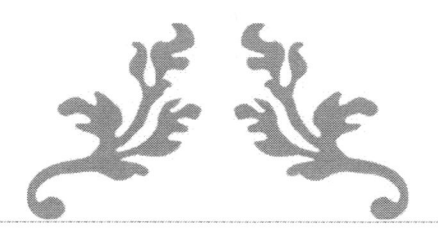

THE PARTNER I PICKED

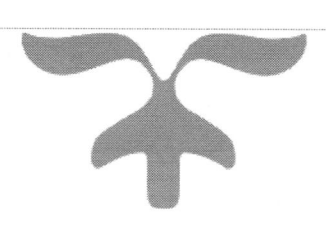

🙠 *The partner I picked* 🙢

CONTENT	AGREE	DISAGREE	DEBATABLE
My ex was open and could take constructive criticism.			
My ex could be described as a kind and warm person.			
My ex always tried to find a positive side of a situation.			
My ex did not beat around the bush, and my ex was very direct.			
My ex was very affectionate.			
Whenever my ex was given a task, they used appropriate checks and balance systems, due diligence and thoroughness.			
My ex could be described as unselfish.			
My ex was fun and engaged in activities outside my comfort zone.			
My ex was not just tunnel visioned with my own values and way of thinking. My ex could put myself in someone else's shoes even if it completely differs from view.			
My ex was self-disciplined, driven, and ambitious.			
My ex was not lazy.			
My ex did not procrastinate.			
My ex has been in control of situations.			

CONTENT	AGREE	DISAGREE	DEBATABLE
My ex was where they wanted to be financially in life.			
My ex was where they wanted to be emotionally in life.			
My ex had done enough work on my issues.			
My ex wanted someone.			
My ex was very patient.			
If my ex wants to date me, they would be exactly who they were.			
My ex considered my life to be in order.			
My ex was shallow.			
My ex was vein.			
My ex needed financial security to feel loved.			
It was easy for my ex to be trusted.			
My ex thought compromise was the same as submitting.			
My ex thought my way of thinking was better at solving problems than most people.			
My ex could be described as condescending.			
My ex was humble, modest, and shy.			
My ex required acknowledgment and validation.			
My ex said I did not need acknowledgement or validation, but it bothered me when I did not get it from my partner.			

CONTENT	AGREE	DISAGREE	DEBATABLE
My ex was sexually open to trying new things with me.			
When my ex was in love, my ex was on a high.			
When a relationship did not work out, my ex was devastated to my core.			
My ex wants my relationship to end happily ever after.			
My ex got bored easily if my partner did not stimulate me constantly.			
My ex was reserved, low energy and not overly animated.			
My ex was passionate, intense and externalized emotionally often.			
My ex was self-conscious, so my ex looked deep into what people may really think, feel or say about me.			
My ex was impulsive and unpredictable.			
My ex had anxiety that required me to explain to my partner that they needed to be mindful of my triggers, mood swings, and irrational responses at times.			
My ex did not like have been vulnerable.			
When I showed my ex vulnerability; it made me know that they really care			
My ex needed my space to be alone without having to explain to my partner what my ex had gone through.			

CONTENT	AGREE	DISAGREE	DEBATABLE
My ex got angry, said things that didn't really mean and felt bad about it often.			
My ex was sometimes emotionally unstable.			
My ex was secure, confident and completely authentic.			
My ex often experiences jealousy.			
My ex wanted my son or daughter to date, marry and have children with a person liked.			
My ex was honest with others.			
My ex was honest with himself/herself.			

Review the questions and answers you just selected. Answer the series of questions below about your choices.

What emotions did you feel as you were answering the questions?

....
....
....
....
....

How honest were you with your answers?

....
....
....
....
....

Did you struggle with your responses?

....
....
....
....
....

What did the answers reveal?

....
....
....
....

Explain in detail what you realized about yourself, what you have to offer, what you could improve on and what you plan to do about your realizations.

....
....
....
....
....
....
....
....
....
....
....
....
....

What role do you think the answers played in your past and previous relationships?

....
....
....
....
....
....
....
....
....
....
....

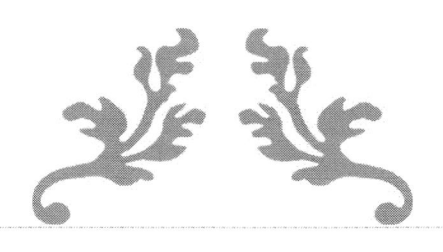

MY FUTURE PARTNER

My Future Partner

CONTENT	AGREE	DISAGREE	DEBATABLE
I want a partner who is open and can take constructive criticism.			
I want a partner who can be described as a kind and warm person.			
I want a partner who always tries to find a positive side of a situation.			
I want a partner who does not beat around the bush, which is very direct.			
I want a partner who is not lazy and who spends energy doing, not pretending to do.			
When and if my partner is given a task, my partner can see it through and use appropriate checks and balance systems, due diligence, and thoroughness.			
I want a partner who can be described as unselfish.			
I want a partner who is fun and engages in activities outside my comfort zone.			
I want a partner who is not just tunnel vision with my own values and way of thinking. Who can put me in someone else's shoe even if it completely differs from view?			
I want a partner who is self-disciplined, driven and ambitious.			
I want a partner who is not lazy.			
I want a partner who does not procrastinate.			

CONTENT	AGREE	DISAGREE	DEBATABLE
I want a partner who prefers to be in control of a situation.			
I want a partner who is where I want to be financially in life.			
I want a partner who is where I want to be emotionally in life.			
I want a partner who has done enough work on my issues.			
I want a partner who wants someone.			
I want a partner who needs someone.			
If my partner were to date me again, I would be exactly whom they will love.			
I want a partner who considers my life to be in order.			
I want a partner who is shallow.			
I want a partner who is a vein.			
I want a partner who needs financial security to feel love.			
It is easy for me to trust.			
I want a partner who thinks compromise is the same as submitting.			
I want a partner who thinks my way of thinking is better at solving problems than most people.			
I want a partner who could be described as condescending.			
I want a partner who is humble, modest, and shy.			
I want a partner who requires acknowledgement and validation.			

CONTENT	AGREE	DISAGREE	DEBATABLE
I want a partner who says I do not need acknowledgement or validation, but it bothers me when I do not get it from my partner.			
I want a partner who is sexually open to trying new things with me.			
When my partner is in love, I am on a high.			
When a relationship doesn't work out, my partner is devastated to my core.			
I want a partner who wants my relationship to end happily ever after.			
I want a partner who gets bored easily if they don't stimulate me constantly.			
I want a partner who is reserved, low energy and not overly animated.			
I want a partner who is passionate intense.			
I want a partner who is Self-conscious so they look deep into what people may really think, feel or say about me.			
I want a partner who is impulsive and unpredictable.			
I want a partner who has anxiety that requires me to explain to them that they need to be mindful of my triggers, mood swings, and irrational responses at times.			
I want a partner who does not like to be vulnerable.			

CONTENT	AGREE	DISAGREE	DEBATABLE
I want a partner who allows me to show vulnerability			
I want a partner who allows me to be alone without asking what I am going through or feeling like I am neglecting them.			
I want a partner who does not get angry, says things they don't really like and feels bad about it after.			
I want a partner who is emotionally stable			
I want a partner who is secure, confident and completely authentic.			
I want a partner who is not jealous.			
I want a partner whom I would want my son or daughter to date, marry and have children with a person of their character			
I want a partner who is honest with others and themselves.			

Review the questions and answers you just selected. Answer the series of questions below about your choices.

What emotions did you feel as you were answering the questions?

....
....
....
....
....

How honest were you with your answers?

....
....
....
....
....

Did you struggle with your responses?

....
....
....
....
....

What did the answers reveal?

....
....
....
....
....

Explain in detail what you realized about yourself, what you have to offer, what you could improve on and what you plan to do about your realizations.

....
....
....
....
....
....
....
....
....
....
....
....
....
....

What role do you think the answers played in your past and previous relationships?

....
....
....
....
....
....
....
....
....
....

CONJUNCTION JUNCTION, WHAT'S YOUR FUNCTION? IS IT DYSFUNCTION

FATHER'S DAY

Today is Father's Day.
We are together under the sun
but apart by miles and lives.
Not nine,
just one,
which you were to guide me through,
but you didn't.
Now what I have
on this Father's Day are
childhood memories
that I cling to,
and my memories sing
in attempt
to hold on to
the parts of you
that I held dear.
My bliss
now only remiss
to soothe the fact

I am your fatherless Child,
still gentle, meek, and mild,
mourning the death of
a father still alive
but dead to my mind and skin
because of the ultimate sin

Committed by you,
who gave me life,
and took my freedom,
imprisoned me
with repressed memories
of betrayal, abandonment, and
daddy issues
spilled over into
bad choices of what a man
should be
For me,
to me,
and with me.

Like a lost lamb,
I wandered into
the wilderness
of wolves not sheep.

Danger surrounded me
while you sleep with
a dead daughter
still fighting
for the life you took

So many missed lessons of
how to duplicate
what should have

been indicative of
unconditional love.
Instead, I always fear that
the other shoe will drop,
and the rug will be pulled
out from my feet
like you did my sheets
when you took all
my Father's Days
and
my one last belief
that
there could be hope
in one man
who would,
and should always
protect me.

Like a thief,
you robbed me
of jewels
that I can
never replace
and had to learn
to live without.

From The Book from "My Heart and Rage To Yours"
by D'annie Grandison

Often, we can recognize in others what we fail to see within ourselves. We are so used to surviving that what we have survived is often pushed to the back of our minds, suppressed, or ignored. Use the puzzle below to identify and acknowledge some dysfunctions to which you may have been exposed.

```
V I J B C J M D N S X J C O T O Q X B K H T L V J
A I A D D I C T I O N I V R R I U U G F R H O I E
R G O O Z V T R T Q I I B B A E S N L I N K R O E
P E Y L S C C S E F O T A X U K I O P Z B E T L D
H F G Z E Z O V E L E B A G M M K P L Z L O N E T
L H E N U N O S A M A A M L A Q I K Y A P D O N Q
O J Z E A F C T T N O P R H U N X L Q Z T T C C V
Z J L G X K I E D H U D S Y G G P W E I S I M E U
E S T L X O E O C I Y J E O L C N U W B Y K O N J
C I N E N Q N T C E P S E R S I D A N I W Q T N M
Y D I C J M D E G R A D A T I O N I I K L R Q S B
O P M T E U I I J T G W Y I P E U K Z R U G I U F
D B H N P E R F E C T I O N I S M U X S T N L Z O
M I T Y C N E D N E P E D O C U U K T Q O L S T N
A O S R S Y O V Q D Q P U H T B J W O I Y G O C H
N T A R C I Q X H Z S T U S C A O K T I U N U I E
I E B H E S C B O T G N Y Z U R N C N R Y J M L C
P I I X K S D A N V U E S X T U E G D M G I B F N
U T J W C N P E L G I R S H S F G Y F F C D D N E
L A U X E S M E R E L S I U R J K R F W E U O O L
A U O P G U E T C H T N M E B M S I C I T I R C O
T B N E G L E C T T E R P N X A O P C D R U J B I
I G O R V H Z P H S K W O F T K M E Z T K W U M V
O T A K Q B G E S Q I D M H M E K N R I S N F Y D
N W U G W O J W N G Z C F O M V G D A S X V F W M
```

Abuse	Abuse	
Anger	Arguments	
Codependency	Conflict	
Criticism	Degradation	
Disrespect	Domestic	
Fear	Guilt	
Manipulation	Neglect	
Perfectionism	Perfectionism	
Sexual	Shaming	
Triangulation	tripping	
Violation	violence	

Describe below some in detail the effects of dysfunctions within your family. What are some of the behaviors you observed mimic or struggled with in your relationship as a result?

....
....
....
....
....
....
....
....
....
....
....
....
....
....
....
....

Childhood was a war for some of us. It left scars and wounds that can take a lifetime to heal. Many of the issues we deal with in relationships, stem from the dysfunction we experienced in our childhood. Our family dynamics play a significant role in who we are in life as we navigate our way through relationships healed or unhealed

Denise Dixon www.iamdenise.com

If you and your partner grew up around dysfunction, it might show up as one of the behaviors below. Have you seen these behaviors in yourself or your ex? Describe how it showed up and how it played out in your relationships

❧ *Expectations to meet unrealistic standards* ☙

Me: ....
....
....
....

My Ex: ....
....
....
....
....

❧ *Extremely Critical* ☙

Me: ....
....
....
....
....

My Ex: ....
....
....
....

❧ *Settled for unmet needs* ❧

Me: ....
....
....
....
....
....

My Ex: ....
....
....
....
....

❧ *Poor Boundaries* ❧

Me: ....
....
....
....
....
....

My Ex: ....
....
....
....
....
....

❧ Withhold Affection ☙

Me: ....
....
....
....
....
....

My Ex: ....
....
....
....
....

❧ Passive Aggressiveness ☙

Me: ....
....
....
....
....
....

My Ex: ....
....
....
....
....

❧ *Depression and anxiety* ☙

Me: ....
....
....
....
....

My Ex: ....
....
....
....
....

❧ *Unable to control temper* ☙

Me: ....
....
....
....
....

My Ex: ....
....
....
....
....

❧ Abusive ☙

Me: ....
....
....
....
....

My Ex: ....
....
....
....
....

❧ Neglect ☙

Me: ....
....
....
....
....

My Ex: ....
....
....
....
....

❧ Disrespectful ❧

Me: ....
....
....
....
....

My Ex: ....
....
....
....
....
....

❧ Mock, Talk Down To, or Shut Down ❧

Me: ....
....
....
....

My Ex: ....
....
....
....
....

❧ *Substance abuse* ☙

Me: ....
....
....
....
....

My Ex: ....
....
....
....
....
....

❧ *Drawn to Chaos, Drama, or Theatrics* ☙

Me: ....
....
....
....
....

My Ex: ....
....
....
....
....
....

❧ People Pleasing ☙

Me: ....
....
....
....
....

My Ex: ....
....
....
....
....

❧ Manipulation and or Lies ☙

Me: ....
....
....
....
....

My Ex: ....
....
....
....
....

What is the probability of your relationships succeeding based on your responses? If so, why, or why not?

....
....
....
....
....
....
....
....
....
....

What role has your exposure to dysfunction played in your relationships?

....
....
....
....
....
....

Are you healed enough to not expose someone to your wounds from dysfunction?

....
....
....
....
....
....

Are you healed enough to recognize being pulled into someone else's unhealed wounds from dysfunction?

……………………………………………………………………………………………
……………………………………………………………………………………………
……………………………………………………………………………………………
……………………………………………………………………………………………
……………………………………………………………………………………………
……………………………………………………………………………………………
……………………………………………………………………………………………
……………………………………………………………………………………………

What role did dysfunction play in your last relationships?

……………………………………………………………………………………………
……………………………………………………………………………………………
……………………………………………………………………………………………
……………………………………………………………………………………………
……………………………………………………………………………………………
……………………………………………………………………………………………
……………………………………………………………………………………………
……………………………………………………………………………………………
……………………………………………………………………………………………
……………………………………………………………………………………………
……………………………………………………………………………………………
……………………………………………………………………………………………
……………………………………………………………………………………………
……………………………………………………………………………………………

KNOWING IS HALF THE BATTLE

The longest and most harmful symptom of dysfunction is prolonged ignorance of its affect and effect. We cannot change the past, but we are mindful and aware of our behavioral patterns and chose the path we will take, knowing what is happening to us now as it occurs.

Feeling bad after the fact is not a part of the healing process, not for you and not for the person you want to be with. It is not healthy for you to experience apologizing, expressing regret, and failing to work on changing behaviors, nor is it healthy for you to subject someone or yourself to these behaviors.

When you are amid the feeling, reaction or response, this is where you can change the behavior, challenge your core beliefs or inner narratives and then take an approach from choice and not predetermine responses.

Review and complete the following sections below. Use the bold areas as tools and identify your internal processing on the provided lines

Decide what you want: In a disagreement, what is the most important thing you need for you to feel peaceful or be contented?

....
....
....

1) ***Identify expectations and where they are coming from:*** What are you most disappointed by, and where does this disappointment come from?

....
....
....

2) ***Uncover your automatic thought:*** What are the thoughts that come to your mind, the ones you say inside your head when you are upset, disappointed, betrayed and or abandoned?

....
....
....

3) ***Identify patterns of limited thinking:*** What loop of thoughts surround your mind that prevents you from agreeing or seeing the other person's point of view?

....
....
....

4) ***Recognize where the pain is coming from:*** Pain comes from somewhere. What does the pain feel like when you are in the midst of conflict or disagreement? What other times or occasions does it feel like?

   ....
   ....
   ....

5) ***Observe yourself:*** Look at yourself, how do you act? Imagine someone else in the same situation with your same response, is it acceptable? Is it healthy? Is it mature?

   ....
   ....
   ....

6) ***Navigate your thoughts:*** What makes you boil inside? What is this about? What emotion sums it up best?

   ....
   ....
   ....

7) ***Identify your worry:*** What do you stand to lose if you lose the argument? What are you worrying that you will be denied or forced to feel?

   ....
   ....
   ....

8) ***Stop the thoughts that do not serve the moment***: Everyone can go on and on, and one with their feelings, thoughts, and views; however, not all of them serve you. Have you recognized the ones that do not serve you?

....
....
....

9) ***Identify your core belief and challenge it***: What does it mean or feel like when your core belief is challenged? Is your core belief a healthy one or a maladaptive one, developed out of survival?

....
....
....

10) ***Acknowledge your feelings:*** If you feel bad in any way, do not deny, hide or run away from it, cry when you're supposed to cry. Striving to feel good all the time is not a goal that can always be reached. How do you acknowledge your feelings when you are in the midst of unwanted emotions?

....
....
....

11) ***Imagine how you would want someone to treat you***: How often do you remove yourself from what you are feeling, and imagine how the other person is feeling, could feel, could be triggered by or may be struggling with? Do you have the ability to remove yourself entirely and think about how you would want to be treated if you were feeling like how the other person may be feeling?

....
....
....

12) ***Detach if necessary:** Do you have an overwhelming need to finalize or solve the issue at hand in every situation, or can you walk away, stick a pin, detach if necessary or must everything be solved in order for you to have peace?*

   ....
   ....
   ....

13) ***Refuse to appease your inner child***: Do you feel like you must make yourself feel the thing you never felt when you were a child in a similar circumstance and as a result, do you feel like you should give yourself the gratification you were denied?

   ....
   ....
   ....

14) ***Don't dish out what you cannot take:*** They say, "hurt people, hurt people." Are you hurt, and do you hurt people as a result of that?

   ....
   ....
   ....

15) ***Maintain healthy boundaries:*** Do you loosen your boundaries at times for others and then expect the same in return? Do you loosen your boundary to be liked or to please people?

   ....
   ....
   ....

16) ***Respect your partner's boundaries:*** When your partner marks boundaries, do you feel bad about that? Do boundaries from a partner feel like rejection, isolation, or abandonment?

   ....
   ....
   ....

17) ***Being okay with being wrong or disagreed with:*** How does it feel when you are told that you are wrong or when you feel wrong? When someone disagrees with you, does it make you angry on the inside and then everyone after that feeling is affected by that feeling?

   ....
   ....
   ....

18) ***Do not avoid or run away from your shame:*** know how you feel when you feel shame in your mind or body?

   ....
   ....
   ....

19) ***Practice forgiving yourself:*** Identify which of the above has been the biggest struggle for you to practice when you are in a relationship

   ....
   ....
   ....
   ....
   ....
   ....

MOVING FORWARD: THE TOP OF ONE MOUNTAIN IS THE BOTTOM OF ANOTHER

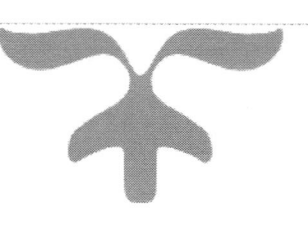

❦ *FADE AWAY* ❧

I like FLOWERS

but I don't

buy them often

they FADE

and when they do

because

they are FLOWERS

I am reminded

why I don't like

what I like so much

⁂ LET US MOVE FORWARD, NOW WHAT ⁂

A relationship needs to be healthy in order for you to grow and thrive. It is also important that you can contribute to someone's growth and not their perpetuated dysfunction, in other words, what you do not want for yourself should not be for someone else.

Complete the section below whether or not the trait is important to you and for you. Explain why or why you do not want your next partner to possess this trait. It is important to hear yourself recognize, identify, and acknowledge that these are things that are important to you and for you to be in your definition of a good or healthy relationship.

Do you want someone who possesses these traits? How important is it to and for you? Why?

Pay attention to the little things

....

....

....

Get along with my friends and family

....

....

....

Give me their undivided attention when we are engaging

....

....

....

❧ LET US MOVE FORWARD, NOW WHAT ❧

You can communicate with them freely

....
....
....

You can agree to disagree

....
....
....

Similar core values

....
....
....

Great communicator

....
....
....

Compromising

....
....

Great Listener

....
....
....

LET US MOVE FORWARD, NOW WHAT

Supportive

....
....
....

Respectful

....
....
....

Romantic

....
....
....

Trustworthy

....
....

Emotional security

....
....

Financial security

....
....
....

LET US MOVE FORWARD, NOW WHAT

Forgiving

....
....
....

Acceptance

....
....
....

Healthy family relationships

....
....
....

Good conflict resolution skills

....
....
....

Accountability

....
....

Sense of humor

....
....
....

LET US MOVE FORWARD, NOW WHAT

Sincerity

....
....
....

Chemistry

....
....
....

Adventurousness

....
....
....

Passionate

....
....
....

Focused

....
....
....

Shared Interests

....
....

LET US MOVE FORWARD, NOW WHAT

Stability

....
....
....

Affectionate

....
....
....

Motivating

....
....
....

Honest

....
....
....

Humble

....
....
....

Grateful

....
....

ঌ*LET US MOVE FORWARD, NOW WHAT* ঌ

Joyful

....
....
....

Smiles or laugh

....
....
....

Confident

....
....
....

Secure

....
....
....

Fair

....
....

Peaceful

....
....

❧ LET US MOVE FORWARD, NOW WHAT ❧

Religious

....
....
....

Spiritual

....
....
....

Empathetic

....
....
....

Kind

....
....
....

Thoughtful

....
....

Gentle

....
....
....

LET US MOVE FORWARD, NOW WHAT

Appreciative

....
....
....

Open

....
....
....

Sensitive

....
....
....

Independent

....
....
....

Grounded

....
....
....

Compassionate

....
....

Now That I Know What I Want, Here Is My Promise To Myself. Dear Me Letter

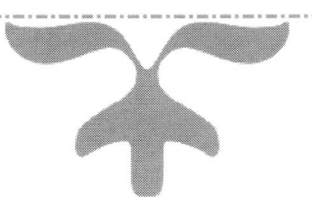

DEAR ME,

❧ *Wrap Up* ❦

Understanding who we are and how we came to be the person we are at present is a lifelong pursuit. In that pursuit, a relationship is often the place where the limitation of our beliefs or the unresolved wounds shows up. Sometimes it's not easy to pick the moth from your own eye, but if we are unable, to be honest with ourselves, then how can we be honest with someone else?

A break-up can be devastating, but what is more devastating is when we learn nothing about ourselves because of it. As the cliché goes, some people are in our life for a reason, a season, or a lifetime. Regardless of the time span, we are at a greater advantage when we understand ourselves and the role we play in what happens to and for us.

As much as we want to be ready for a relationship, we aren't always. The goal is to be able to look within yourself and know for sure. We're all works in progress, but it's ultimately our responsibility to enter relationships in a healthy enough state to recognize what works and what doesn't.

On the pages below, reflect on what you have learned, discovered, or forced to confront. How will this change your pattern moving forward? Are you ready for a relationship? Why or why not?

If you believe that you could benefit from continued healing from you past relationship. Please join us at our Breakup School. Courses are first come first serve and limited spots are available. Additionally, individual sessions are available. We offer a full course which is a more in-depth version of this workbook. We also offer retreats, online and in person sessions and a fully immersive experience.

Notes:

Notes:

Thank you for purchasing one of our Books, Workbooks, or Journals. We are honored you chose us for this part of your journey. If you continue the journey with us please reorder the same or one of our other products.

Made in the USA
Columbia, SC
06 February 2024